Wolf in the Sheepfold

ROBERT P CARROLL

Wolf in the Sheepfold

**THE BIBLE AS A PROBLEM FOR
CHRISTIANITY**

First published in Great Britain 1991
SPCK
Holy Trinity Church
Marylebone Road
London NW1 4DU

© Robert P. Carroll 1991

All rights reserved. No part of this book may be
reproduced or transmitted in any form or by any means,
electronic or mechanical, including photocopying,
recording, or by any information storage and retrieval
system, without permission in writing
from the publisher.

British Library Cataloguing in Publication Data

Carroll, Robert P.
  Wolf in the sheepfold : the Bible as a
  problem for Christianity.
  1. Christianity. Scriptures
  I. Title
  220.13

  ISBN 0-281-04525-9

Printed in Great Britain by
The Longdunn Press Ltd, Bristol

For Robert Davidson
in celebration of his years as Professor
in the University of Glasgow
and as personal colleague
1972–1991

Stupid clergymen appeal quite directly to a Bible passage directly understood . . .

Søren Kirkegaard

What is the point of the arts of reading and criticism as long as the ecclesiastical interpretation of the Bible, Protestant as well as Catholic, is cultivated as ever?

Friedrich Nietzsche

There is no document of civilization which is not at the same time a document of barbarism.

Walter Benjamin

A figure like Ecclesiast,
Rugged and luminous, chants in the dark
A text that is an answer, although obscure.

Wallace Stevens

The Bible is clearly a major element in our own imaginative tradition, whatever we may think we believe about it. It insistently raises the question: Why does this huge, sprawling, tactless book sit there inscrutably in the middle of our cultural heritage like the 'great Boyg' or sphinx in *Peer Gynt*, frustrating all our efforts to walk around it?

Northrop Frye

Contents

Preface

It is with a deep sense of faith – *mauvaise foi* I suspect – that I release this book on a mercifully restricted public. Having committed myself to writing it some time ago, the closer I got to the actual writing of it the less I felt that I could or should. After more than thirty years of studying the Bible in various languages I still find that my understanding of it and my views on it *qua* book seem to change all the time. Little of what I want to say about the Bible ever survives my saying it without my wanting to abandon what has just been said. This book belongs firmly to that category. It is my actual response to the request of my editor at SPCK, Philip Law, for a book, and reflects my deep puzzlement at the role the Bible plays in theology. Between the Bible and what theologians do with and to it lies the astonishment which has fuelled this book. They have belled the book, and now that they have domesticated it, it gives an uncertain sound. My book is an attempt to sketch and explore some of the facets of the ecclesiastical captivity of the Bible, but without any plans for an escape from the theological Colditz to which the Bible has been condemned.

I have dedicated this modest book to my colleague Robert Davidson because its appearance in public should coincide with his retirement in 1991. For almost twenty years we have shared the teaching of the Bible in the University of Glasgow and, whatever the fundamental theological differences between us, they have been most cordial years. As a token of respect and affection I hope he will accept this book in the spirit in which it is given – as the will for the deed.

ROBERT P. CARROLL
Glasgow
September 1990

Introduction

The author of man's canons is man.

Wallace Stevens

A text always has several epochs and reading must resign itself to that fact.

Jacques Derrida

There is no copyright on the Bible. Various translations and editions of the Bible are the property of different publishing houses, but no one person, community, institution or nation can be said to 'own' the Bible. It is a freelance book, loose in human culture though subject to the canons of time-conditioned cultural production and the necessities of interpretation. Its authors and producers are generally unknown, and the processes whereby it came to have the forms in which we know it are shrouded in legends of the past. At some stage between the fourth and sixth centuries of the Common Era, codexes resembling what we know as the Bible began to make their appearances. Since then it has been an important element in the creation of European culture and has functioned in a variety of religious, intellectual and ideological ways. Whatever its origins may have been in the Oriental world (the ancient Near East), we think of it as a European book because we know it in translated forms reflecting Western values. It is not, of course, a European book at all, but a collection of books from a past not our own and from cultures very different from ours.

Myths about the Bible being a single book and also our *own* book are difficult to dislodge from Western consciousness. Equally hard to change are notions about the book's nature and its at-homeness in our culture. The alienness and 'otherness' of the Bible, along with the fact that it exists in different and distinctive forms for various religious communities, are some of the main concerns of this book. This, however, is not a scholarly work but a lightweight book consisting of a few exploratory sketches intended to make the reader reflect on some facts about and interpretations of the discrete Bibles of Western culture. It is not a book of academic scholarship because I have assiduously avoided the footnote, the learned disquisition on technical subjects, and the well-balanced consideration of every viewpoint under the sun. Rather it is an exploration into what *I see* as being some of the main problems in using the Bible in the contemporary world. I write from the position of a scholar in the modern academy whose main work deals with the ancient past and the cultures which produced the Bible. But I have written for the non-expert rather than for my fellow scholars, who will learn nothing from this book. Having taught the Hebrew Bible, with occasional forays into the Greek Bible and the New Testament, and the English Bible, for twenty-three years now (cf. Jeremiah 25.3) in a secular university (though one whose origins have a papal dimension), I have written this book as simply as I could in order to clear some of the lumber out of my head and to sort out what I regard as being the problems of the Bible for theology. The brevity of the volume necessarily restricts the areas of difficulty which can be scrutinized, but I hope my selection of problems will prove illuminating.

The Bible is a profoundly problematical collection of books in many senses – religious, cultural, political, intellectual, moral, ethical and aesthetic – as well as posing problems for modern strategies of reading (Marxian, feminist, philosophical, postmodernist, etc.). While I shall focus on the central problems of reading the Bible today, I shall not undertake any investigation of such contemporary ways of reading the Bible; as the libraries of the West are overstocked with all manner of volumes on the subject, I shall content myself in this book with the simplest and most non-technical analysis of certain aspects of the Bible. It is intended for the puzzled Bible-reader: not in order to resolve the puzzles but to deepen the sense of puzzlement and to confirm the reader's good sense in being mystified by the Bible. If reading the Bible does *not* raise profound problems for you as a modern reader, then check with your doctor and enquire about the symptoms of brain-death.

Problems of nomenclature may also puzzle the reader, so a few words may be in order here. The word 'Bible' means the Hebrew Bible to Jews, but something else to Christians. For biblical scholars, Bible means the Hebrew or Greek Bible, with or without the Greek New Testament. To Christians who are monolingual or who have many languages but not Aramaic, Hebrew and Greek, Bible usually means English Bible, *Die Bibel*, *La Bible*, or whatever natural language is spoken. However, Christians are not a uniform group of people. They come in many different forms and denominations, so a Catholic Bible is different from a Protestant Bible. It is different in the senses that there are more books in the Catholic version of what Christians call 'the Old Testament' and that the whole book has a very different history of translation and interpretation.

Nobody can be a Jew, a Catholic *and* a Protestant, so in practice all the different Bibles tend to be regarded as versions of the same book. For working purposes this confusion of the many with the one may not be a serious problem, but it does delude people into thinking that there is only one Bible. On the contrary, there are at least three Bibles and, while they may share many things in common, their differences are significant. My first chapter will attempt to say more about these fundamental variations in the holy books of various religious communities. Perhaps it would be wiser if people spoke of the Bible using a prefix such as the '*Jewish* Bible' or the '*Christian* Bible', with an additional indication of whether '*Christian*' here means 'Catholic' or 'Protestant'. I tend to use the phrase 'Christian Bible' to mean the Catholic one because the changes introduced by the Reformation created the book we know as the Protestant Bible. Just for the record, my own preferences are for the Hebrew Bible and the Greek New Testament, with the Greek Bible as a supplementary for books not to be found in the Hebrew Bible. As the English Bible I use the ecumenical edition (what is sometimes called the Common Bible) of the Revised Standard Version (RSV). There are simply far too many versions in English for any sane person to use them all. So throughout this book I have tended to use the RSV when citing the Bible, though occasionally the RSV text has been tinkered with by me for aesthetic reasons.

One other problem of nomenclature should perhaps be explained for the careful reader. From time to time I use the phrase 'conciliar Christianity'. That is shorthand for the type of Christian religion generated by the great councils of the churches which met from the fourth century onwards. These official gatherings manufactured what we know as 'orthodoxy', so I use the shorthand phrase to indicate to the reader that we are dealing with loaded terms. All such terms are freighted with ideology – as Nietzsche observed, 'there are no facts, only interpretations' – and the wise reader will bear in mind that there were many other Christian communities which did not subscribe to the dogmas of orthodoxy. The diversity of beliefs and practices in the ancient churches has to be recognized, and the stories told by the ideological victors should not be the only tales heard. Such diversity of matters can also be found in the Bibles of different communities, and again the competent reader will be wary of schemes which insist that scripture is somehow a body of unified belief whose meaning is single, definite and fixed. (Good grief, the texts are not even fixed, let alone their meanings!) So the use of the phrase 'conciliar Christianity' includes warnings as well as information and is intended to introduce the reader to some of the subtleties of reading.

Because this book is of an exploratory nature I have not attempted a comprehensive introduction to the history of the reception of the Bible, nor have I tried to return to the past in order to present an account of the Bible in terms of traditional dogmas about sacred scripture. The reader will find here no reliance on beliefs about the inspiration of the Bible, nor serious talk about the Bible being 'the word of God'. Such approaches to the Bible belong to its reception rather than to the books which constitute it. They are beliefs *about* the Bible. As a practitioner of the critical reading approach it is inevitable that my book should regard the Bible as the product of human communities. The production of canons of sacred scripture is a human, an all-too-human, activity. As one of the epigraphs to this introduction observes, 'the author of man's canons is man'. The processes whereby the words of human beings become, with time, identified with the words of the God worshipped in specific communities are complex and often defy historical investigation. Since the rise of critical theology in the modern age, the equating of the human words of scripture with the words of God has been abandoned. A simple reading through of the Bible will demonstrate to any rational reader just why that should be so. The fact that there are still many religious communities who treat the Bible like the Qu'ran and believe it to have been written by God by means of its human authors does not undermine the critical viewpoint. It just makes things more complicated and perhaps more interesting. It also means that there are different levels of reading the Bible. This book comes from the community of scholars; the reader should be aware that there are also communities of faith. The fact that sometimes these different communities overlap and that some people would regard themselves as belonging to both, also complicates matters. But the reader should be careful to read the implicit warning about all books regarded as coming from the gods – such claims are calls to privilege certain texts and to exempt them from critical scrutiny. Beware of all such claims because they tend to privilege particular readings of texts, and often those readings are against the grain of the text.

Much of what follows this introduction has as its subtext (a term used to describe the real concerns of a text which do not appear in the writing of that text) a concern with the ideological manipulation of the Bible. Collections of books, such as the Bible, have many meanings and uses, and over a long period of history those meanings and uses can change quite radically. Such books, when treated as sacred scripture, can be very dangerous indeed. They are very vulnerable to manipulation, and because of the great diversity of what they contain they can be made to serve the powerful as weapons against the weak. Whatever the Bible may say about oppression it has in its time served the interests of the oppressor. Chapters Three and Four try to say something about that aspect of the problem of the Bible. It is not just the *use* of the Bible, but also some of the substantive things in the Bible itself. The Bible, in whatever version, may make a good servant; it can be a bad master. Treating it as the divine word exempt from criticism can blind the eyes to that truth. Also, the Bible contains some appalling practices of an uncivilized nature and nobody should treat these as normative. As Walter Benjamin said, 'there is no document of civilization which is not at the same time a document of barbarism.' The Bible also has its dimension of barbarism, and that is part of what makes it such a problematic book. Better that the book should be seen as part of our past and as a contributor to the good and bad things about modern European society (the Eurocentric concern of this book is an acknowledgement of partial vision and not a reflection of an ideal state of knowledge) than that it should be misunderstood to the point of idolatry. A different and better book might have been written about more positive aspects of the Bible, but it would have been much longer and far more technical. And besides, the world is overflowing with books praising the Bible. There is room for a book about its more negative aspects – hence this one on the Bible as a problem for Christianity.

1
The Book of Books

Hey Snags wots in the bibl'?
wot are the books ov the bible?
Name 'em, don't bullshit ME.

Ezra Pound

It is a truism to say that the Bible is not a book but a collection of books (*ta biblia* –'the books'). Yet most people could be forgiven for thinking of it as one book because since the days of printing it has been represented as a single volume (except for Braille editions). Even when its nature as a collection or congeries of books is acknowledged, or at least known, people still tend to think of it as a unity having one author and one message. These are the illusions of time and familiarity. Not only is the Bible a book made up of many, diverse books, it is also a number of different books, dependent on the reader's perspective. In a very real sense there is no such thing as *the* Bible. There are only Bibles – Hebrew, Christian, Protestant. There is no original Bible, only the different collections of writings associated with very distinctive religious communities. Talk about 'the Bible' borders on the mythical. It is an abstraction which represents no concrete, universal reality. It is an idea which takes different forms in different cultures and communities.

Because readers of the Bible tend to think of their version of the book as having always existed as such, or at least since the beginning of their religious traditions, they are ill-disposed to think of it as something which had a beginning in a time *after* the formation of their religious communities. The earliest Christian communities and churches did not have a Bible. Christian existence predates the Bible by a number of centuries. The great Christian creeds are virtually Bible-free. Of course, many of the earliest churches made use of various writings, and with time some of these writings were incorporated into what was to become one version of the Bible.

Other writings are known to us from the Jewish Bible, though the treatment of these in the book we know as the New Testament is very different from the way they were read by Jews. A plethora of writings was available to the earliest churches and a great many more were produced by them. Yet not all the writings used or created by the churches became part of what subsequently formed the Christian Bible. Important though they may have been in the formation of early Christian thought, many writings disappeared from or were discarded by later Christian communities in their construction of the Christian Bible. We know now of important libraries which were formative in an earlier period (e.g. those at Qumran and Nag Hammadi) but which were lost from sight for many centuries because the evolving churches failed to incorporate them into their canonical writings in the fourth to sixth centuries. Other writings have left only traces in the Christian Bible, or never became sufficiently important for enough communities to become part of that book (e.g. The Book of Enoch). But today many scholars would regard the Qumran literature, the Gnostic gospels, Enoch and various pseudepigraphal writings as absolutely fundamental background information for understanding the New Testament. In many cases this literature was more important in the actual formation of the New Testament than much of what Christians call the Old Testament, because it belongs to the thinking processes which produced much of the New Testament. The Jewish scriptures were of course important for the formation of the New Testament writings, but mostly in the Greek versions of those writings rather than in their original Hebrew or Aramaic forms. But their importance was modified by the fact that the hermeneutic processes used in the New Testament came from the non-canonical literature rather than from the Greek version of the Jewish scriptures.

This combination of different literatures and various hermeneutic frameworks, allied to changing circumstances and emergent situations, not to mention scriptures and writings in translation, makes the composition of Bibles a far more complex matter than is often realized. The existence of different versions of a specific text, either as copies of that text or as translations of it, militates against the notion of an *original* text behind whatever version of the Bible may be regarded as important by a particular religious community. For we have no such thing as an original Bible. We have no originals for any of the books in the Bible (whichever version is preferred). Even that statement is disputable in that it seems to presuppose that it makes sense to talk about 'original texts'. But we have no evidence for such a notion as 'an original text'. All copies of any biblical texts are different. That is the nature of ancient writings and their copies. The production of scrolls was a tiresome and tedious business prone to many mistakes (a glance at a Qumran scroll will prove this point). With the passage of time the Christian communities came to favour the codex form over the scroll form and eventually produced the book form. A scrutiny of a reliable edition of the Greek Septuagint (e.g. the Göttingen Septuagint) or the Greek New Testament will reveal a world of textual recensions and families of texts bearing on the production of a reliable text. But is there an original text behind that reliable text? In the case of the Septuagint we are dealing with a text in translation, and that factor further complicates matters.

The problems of translation

The book which people know as the Bible (whichever version it may be) is, except for the learned scholar, a book in translation. Often that translation is already a translation itself. The Christian Bible is made up of a volume translated from Hebrew into Greek and a smaller volume of Greek writing. That book was eventually translated into Latin which in turn was translated into English – a translation of a translation of a translation! Modern English Bibles (Christian, i.e. Catholic and Protestant) tend to be translated directly from the Hebrew (and from the Greek Septuagint for the variations between Catholic and Protestant Old Testaments) and the Greek (New Testament). But they are still books in translation. Of course it is arguable under certain conditions that the Authorized Version of the English Bible is an English book in its own right. At least it is so for the vast majority of people today and, provided no fantasies are being indulged, it may count as such for religious purposes.

Some important points are being made here. However much at home people may be with their English Bibles, it must always be kept in mind that the Bible is a collection of translations of alien literatures in alien languages from ancient and alien times. Now it is always possible to over-emphasize the sheer alienness of the Bible; but the more common failing has been to forget its alien qualities. In forgetting that the Bible is an essentially alien work (or congeries of alien books) a worse sin has been committed – that of the domestication of the Bible (see Chapter Five below).

Beyond the delusion of domesticity is a more important point about texts in translation. All languages have their own distinctive worlds of expression and understanding, so that when one language is translated into another, those worlds change. The changes may or may not be significant, depending on what is being translated into what. Engineering terms or technical scientific language may translate relatively easily, but poetry and conceptual thought are the dickens to translate (easy and difficult here are relative). All translation changes things, though we could argue for ever about whether such changes are benign or malignant. Matching words, phrases, images and sentences in different languages raises many difficult questions about equivalences and appropriate expressions, not to mention general issues of interpretation. So a work of poetry or literature in translation is always a lesser entity than its original form – though it may be arguable that the degree of inexactitude is tolerable. The Bible cannot escape such strictures about translation. In the case of older versions, where the translation is a translation of a translation, the distance of the work from the original language is even more considerable.

Questions about the advisability of translating the scriptures are part of ancient discussions about the Bible. Jerome, the great translator of most of the Christian Bible into Latin (the Vulgate), debated with Augustine the question of translation as well as the question of inspiration in relation to original or translated languages. Jerome took the view that only the original languages of the Bible were inspired and not the translations, whereas Augustine (with the better logic I think) argued that the Spirit had inspired the Greek translation of the scriptures. Inspired scripture which yields uninspired translation may well be the truth of the matter, but most Christian communities have tended to side with Augustine and treated their version of the Bible (in whatever language) as also inspired. The Jewish practice of translating their texts – the production of the Septuagint was a phenomenal undertaking and unique in the ancient world – presupposed that there was an exactitude of translation from one language into another; though it is worth noting that the Aramaic translations of the Hebrew Bible (the Targums) were more paraphrase than translation (except in the matter of translating *torah*). Islam has always held to the view that the

Qu'ran cannot be translated and remain the Qu'ran. The faithful must learn to read the sacred text in its original Arabic or forgo access to it. That has a logic to it which Jewish and Christian communities have generally denied in practice, if not in theory.

The opacity of the Bible

Whether the Bible is read in Hebrew or in Aramaic paraphrase, in Greek or in Latin, in English or any other language far removed from the original biblical languages, the problems of interpretation and understanding will always remain. For beyond the distortions and deviations of any translation there remains the more fundamental problem of the opacity of the Bible. Augustine, Origen and many other major Christian writers of the early churches knew well the sheer difficulty of reading the Bible (which for them was mainly the Greek or Latin Old Testament). Since the Reformation it has been fashionable to think of the Bible (or its subject matter) as simple. On the contrary, even in translation it is far from simple, and in its original languages much of it is opaque. Perhaps this is true of all language when it relates to the transcendental and seeks to speak of things beyond the margins of our experience. It is certainly often true of poetry, and much of the Bible is poetry. Language which attempts to take us beyond the boundaries of the ordinary into the world of the extraordinary is necessarily and inevitably imprecise. Of course many modern translations of the Bible into English have attempted to get rid of its opacity and to render it comprehensible to a non-reading public. Such attempts must be regarded as folly at some level. Translations can be improved and can be made more accurate – biblical translation could certainly be improved if it were performed by poets and writers endowed with the gift of *Sprachgefühl* (a nice example of an untranslatable word which cannot be improved in translation: roughly it means 'a feel for language'). But such improvements would not necessarily penetrate the opacity of the Bible, though they might well serve the reader better. I cannot imagine, however, that even a better translation of the books of Ezekiel and Revelation would make either book any the more transparent.

Books and talk about the transcendental are necessarily opaque, because if we could clearly understand the divine it would not be the divine – it would be merely something human. Yet the opacity of the Bible goes far beyond just having the divine as its putative subject matter. It is to be found also in its poetic language, its semantic codes and its alien, ancient modes of expression. Open any version of the Bible at any page and problems of interpretation and meaning will hit the reader very quickly. A comparison of different translations will also make this point. Now difficulty in reading is not a rare or unusual experience. Any good book is going to puzzle the reader from time to time. Even the writings of Spinoza, Kant and Heidegger pose problems of meaning for the most competent of readers. But as we go back in time and cross the boundaries of different and ancient languages the difficulties increase. Understanding Aristotle and Plato or Heraclitus and other pre-Socratics is not an easy task. And so it is with the Bible. Being a collection of books, the Bible has many levels of difficulty, as well as material which may be regarded as relatively easy to understand. Stories such as those of Jonah, Judith and Ruth seem to be straightforward, as do so many narratives, but there are also degrees of subtlety in each story which can baffle the reader.

Because the Bible, whatever the version, is sacred scripture for many religious communities and churches, its opacity and its many difficulties are often ignored or subsumed under beliefs about inspiration and the transparency of scripture. Such a collection of diverse books, gathered together over a long period from many different provenances, tends to invite the selection of a few favourite sections, which in turn serves to make the Bible seem a strictly functional book without depth or difficulty. In such social contexts the notion of the Bible as difficult, complex and complicated is regarded as counter-productive and glossed over in favour of a religious reading of the selected parts, which is both simplistic and a violation of the rest of the book. If much of the history of the interpretation of the Bible over the past two thousand years reads more like the rape of the book (to use a metaphor of violation), that is perhaps because its depth and difficulty do not permit it to be used as easily as might at first appear to be the case. Depth, difficulty and diversity are all factors which make the books which constitute the Bible (whichever community's version is under scrutiny) desperately in need of interpretation (*Deutungsbedürftigkeit* is Auerbach's single German word for this necessity). And such a need for interpretation entails interpreters.

A classical statement about this need for interpretation is to be found in the New Testament. There is a story in Acts 8 (verses 26 to 39) about the encounter of the apostle Philip with the Ethiopian eunuch on a desert road. As one of Queen Candace's officials he may be regarded as an educated man, and as a pilgrim to Jerusalem he must be thought of as a pious God-fearer, if not actually Jewish. His wealth may have allowed him to acquire an Isaiah scroll for himself, or the story line may have granted him a scroll in order to develop the argument – as far as interpreting the biblical text goes it is a moot point. Philip encountered the Ethiopian reading (aloud, of course, because that was the normal form of reading until at least the fourth century) towards the end of the scroll and asked him the fundamental question: 'Do you understand what you are reading?' His reply was, in the circumstances, equally foundational: 'How can I, unless some one guides me' (vv. 30–31). Lacking someone to show him the way (the sense of the Greek text here) he was bemused by the text.

This is the paradigm of Bible reading, perhaps of all textual encounters – the need to be shown *how* to read (i.e. to interpret or understand) the biblical text. For the Ethiopian the site of confusion in the text was a section of Isaiah which we know as chapter 53 verses 7 to 8 (chapter and verse divisions of the Bible belong to a period at least a thousand years after the formation of the different canons). As a shrewd reader of the text the Ethiopian could see the obvious problems of reference in the piece cited. What, or rather who, was the prophet speaking about? Any and all readers of Isaiah 53 even to this day will ask that most obvious of questions – though one effect of the Acts 8 story has been to short-circuit the question by foreclosing too quickly on an answer to it. Philip used the occasion to inform the Ethiopian of the good news of Jesus, beginning with the Isaiah piece.

A number of important principles about reading the Bible are to be found in this story. Apart from the most significant one about requiring a skilled interpreter to guide one through the meaning, two others may be noted here. The Ethiopian's second question to Philip implies the ambiguity of the text. Philip's response to that question resolves the ambiguity in line with his own hermeneutic framework, derived from the good news (gospel) of Jesus. These two principles are very important for the understanding of biblical writings: texts are capable of more than one meaning, and in order to resolve that ambiguity a framing principle of interpretation must be imposed on the text. The hermeneutics of the reader is fundamental to the understanding of the text. The Ethiopian lacked a hermeneutic and therefore could not understand what he was reading. Philip already possessed a hermeneutic which enabled him to read that specific text in a certain way and answer the Ethiopian's questions to the mutual satisfaction of both parties. The meaning of the Isaiah text remains open (i.e. ambiguous) but Philip's evangelical reading of it closed it for the Ethiopian and led to his baptism. A nice combination of text and reader, interpreter and hermeneutic, situation (desert and water) and possibility, produces a paradigm of interpretation. Texts do not mean anything by themselves but require situations to which interpreters bring their own hermeneutics in order to resolve specific questions of interpretation. Different occasions, different situations, different questions and different interpreters will generate different meanings from ostensibly the same texts.

So to difficulty and diversity must be added ambiguity and open-endedness of meaning, as well as reader's situation and interpreter's hermeneutic, in constructing the conditions under which the Bible may be read and understood. Every one of these factors contributes significantly to the many different readings possible for any phrase, line, verse or section. These factors, when combined with different translations and distinctive religious traditions, yield further possibilities of meaning and understanding. The modes of discourse used when reading the Bible determine the kind of meaning derived from or imposed on the text. Traditional words such as 'exegesis' and 'eisegesis' function as shorthand terms for these ways of reading texts, but the matter is more complicated than either of these terms suggests. And the complications are compounded when the different and differing religious systems in which various versions of the Bible exist are taken into account. Jews, Catholics and Protestants have different Bibles, distinctive hermeneutic systems and their own range of peculiar religious communities, which transform apparently similar texts into very different books.

Which Bible?

It may be thought by some people that the essential difference between the Bibles of Jews, Catholics and Protestants is merely a matter of degree; the Jews have the smallest book and the Catholics the biggest one, with the Protestants somewhere in between. This is not simply a naïve viewpoint but a wrong one. What Jews have in the Hebrew Bible is a collection of books (the precise number varies according to different systems of counting) in Hebrew and Aramaic, in which the first five books (*Torah*) dominate the life of orthodox Jews. More important for Jewish thinking than the Hebrew Bible are the writings of later periods on the *Torah*, especially embodied in the Talmuds (both Babylonian and Jerusalem) and a huge literature of narrative and commentary on the Hebrew Bible. The rabbinic principles of interpretation of that Bible have been developed over many centuries and determine how the book is read. But more significant than the book is the life of the community and the maintenance of Jewish ways of life. How a Jew relates to the Hebrew Bible and reads it are very different modes of perception and practice from how Christians might relate to it or its equivalent. Jews and Christians do *not* share the same book nor do they share similar principles of interpretation. Their ways of life and worship have little in common except the most superficial of resemblances. A glance at a page of Talmud in comparison to a page from a Christian biblical commentary of the same period will speak volumes of difference between the two. They are worlds apart. The origins, history, experience, outlook and aspirations of Jewish and Christian communities are so different that any imagined similarities can only be misleading.

I have emphasized the differences between Jews and Christians in order to underline important distinctions between the Bibles often thought to be the same. Of course there is a level at which in the past Jews and Christians had some things in common. Jesus was a Jew, and many of the earliest Christian communities had Jewish members. Certain linguistic and conceptual elements in Christian thought owe something to those Jewish origins. But Talmudic and orthodox Judaism (or Judaism*s* as Jacob Neusner has taught us to think of it) as we know it, belongs to a period after the time of Jesus and after the destruction of Jerusalem by the Romans in the first century of the Common Era. So while Jews and Christians may share some roots in some sense, the fully grown trees have turned out to be very different in nature. The conventional epithetic description 'Judeo-Christian' is very much a myth in the worst sense of that word. It confuses more than it illuminates and it seriously misleads at every important juncture of thought. (I should say, however, just in case any reader makes the serious mistake of reading what is not between the lines here: this insistence on the difference between Jews and Christians, especially in relation to holy books, has got nothing to do with notions of superiority or inferiority. It has solely to do with difference.)

When the socio-political conditions in which many Jewish communities lived changed under the influence of the ancient Greek empire, it became necessary to translate the sacred writings into Greek. Over a number of centuries this necessity produced the Septuagint. A magnificent intellectual achievement, that large-scale translation project resulted in an enlarged version of the Hebrew Bible. That is, it contained more books than were in the Hebrew version and therefore represented a rather different canon of scripture (known as the Alexandrian canon). A further difference between the two was a different order of books: in the Hebrew canon the books of the prophets follow immediately after the books of Kings and thereby form the 'latter' prophets to the 'former' prophets of Joshua-Judges-Samuel-Kings. In the Septuagint the book of Ruth follows that of Judges, and the books of Kings (i.e. Samuel and Kings) are followed by the books of Chronicles, 1 Esdras, 2 Esdras (Ezra-Nehemiah), Esther, Judith, Tobit, and the four books of Maccabees. The Hebrew Bible has the prophets followed by the book of Psalms, then Job, Proverbs, Ruth, Song of Songs, Qoheleth (Ecclesiastes), Lamentations, Esther, Daniel, Ezra, Nehemiah and the books of Chronicles. In the Septuagint, after the histories come the poetic and prophetic books. The poetic books include the Wisdom of Solomon and the Psalms of Solomon as well as Ben Sirach or Ecclesiasticus, none of which is to be found in the Hebrew Bible. Among the prophetic books of the Septuagint are included the book of Daniel, additions to Jeremiah or writings associated with that prophet (Baruch, the Letter of Jeremiah and the book of Lamentations attributed to Jeremiah), Susanna, Bel and the Dragon (associated with Daniel), and there are some differences of order among the minor prophets (the Book of the Twelve). It should be obvious from these listings that the Hebrew Bible and the Septuagint are different in many ways. The fundamental differences of language, translation and reinterpretation compound the distinctions between the two Bibles. As our current versions of the Septuagint are made up from many different manuscripts and families of Greek texts, the matter is much more complex than my simple outline indicates.

The sacred writings used by the writers of the New Testament approximate more to the Septuagint (and other Greek versions) than they do to the Hebrew scriptures, and so reflect the world of Hellenistic thought. In the early centuries of the Christian churches a wide range of literature was used by various writers, and it is impossible to generalize about what constituted scripture for any particular community. For some writers (for example Ignatius of Antioch), the notion of scripture was unimportant whereas for others, (such as Clement of Alexandria) everything written appears to have been authoritative. Between these two poles of opinion and practice various individuals and communities may be allotted a position. The rediscovery of the Gnostic gospels over the past century has revealed a much more diverse picture of the ancient Christian communities, in which difference and variety had greater roles to play than is sometimes allowed for in popular histories of Christian origins. After the Constantinian revolution in the political fortunes of some of the churches, certain forms of Christian belief and practice became favoured over others. No doubt under the influence of Marcion and in reaction to his radical views about sacred writings there developed movements towards producing a Christian canon of scripture, which was to unite some churches and exclude others. In the late fourth century some consensus among certain communities developed in the construction of the New Testament. Allied to councils and creeds in the fourth and fifth centuries the Christian Bible began to emerge, complete with a dogmatic framework of interpretation. This Bible consisted of the Septuagint and the New Testament as we know it (i.e. important Christian writings were excluded from the final canonical collection). It was to take centuries for this Bible to become the sole orthodox canon, and then only after the imperial power had contributed to the annihilation of ancient Christian communities and writings.

Canons are about struggle and community conflict. They are also about the triumph of ideology. Ideological conflicts of the past often leave their only trace in what is included in or excluded from the list of canonical writings. To the modern reader puzzled by the contents page of a modern Bible and wondering why some curious entries appear on it and others not (this is a remarkably well-read modern reader), one can only talk about 'battles long ago'. The Jewish canonization processes avoided apocalypses like the plague, and the Christian canonization processes fled from Gnostic writings. Also, the construction of controlling hermeneutic principles helped to make the reading of the canon conform to the practices of the communities using it. What is contained in a canonical list is less important than the hermeneutic framework used to control its interpretation. Hence the Christian churches were able to go on using the Greek version of Jewish scriptures (even if now translated into Latin) because they read these writings in a christological and allegorical manner. The practices and beliefs which separated Christians very clearly from Jewish communities could be reconciled by means of a series of complex reinterpretations with scriptures which prescribed Jewish practices (here Origen was the great master of translating Jewish scripture into Christian allegory). A reading of the prophets as being predominantly predictive (a Qumran practice) and essentially messianic (a view taken by some Jews) facilitated the appropriation of the prophets in the service of Jesus the Messiah. Difficulties and ambiguities in the Jewish scriptures allowed Christian exegetes to develop their own readings of the text in support of a Christian viewpoint.

The subject of canons and canonic processes is much more complex than I have set out here, but space does not permit a proper treatment of it nor is it central to the main concerns of this book. If I were to pursue the complexities of each individual Christian writer's treatment of what Christians came to call 'the old testament' (in contradistinction to the new testament) this would be a very different book. What is important for my argument is the fact that in adapting and adopting the Septuagint the earliest Christian writers had already made a number of moves away from the Hebrew Bible (moves also made no doubt by various communities of Hellenistic Jews). Combined with their different hermeneutic principles and the emergence of the New Testament and other Christian writings, these factors make the Christian Bible (Septuagint plus New Testament or both in the Vulgate translation) something very different from the Hebrew Bible with additions. As has already been shown, Jews and Christians do not share a Bible (or half a Bible) in common. They have some books which bear a family resemblance to each other but this resemblance is radically altered when the interpretative frameworks are changed and the life situations in which the translated texts are read are different. When the New Testament is combined with the Old Testament a very different book is created. The centre shifts, and the original book is incorporated as a prologue or first volume rather than as a book in its own right. The meanings attached to the writings in the first book are necessarily changed because they take on a new signification determined by the second book. These changes are further highlighted if communities using the first book survive and develop very different strategies of reading from those employed by Christian communities for their new two-volume book.

The differences between Jewish and Christian communities in their subsequent developments and in their interpretative control of their sacred books were less than subtle and may be traced by any competent historian of late antiquity and early medieval European society. Within Europe the development of Western Christendom (for the sake of brevity I must omit any consideration of Eastern Byzantine Christianity where things were arranged somewhat differently) included the use of the Vulgate Bible for a further thousand years until the Protestant Reformation in Germany and Geneva introduced a modification of the Bible. For some centuries before Luther and Calvin emerged as reformers in the sixteenth century there had been various movements across Europe to translate the Bible into different vernacular languages. After the disruption of the Catholic Church by the different reforming movements the Christian Bible became more available in different languages, and a Protestant or reformed version of that Bible was developed. This version differed from the Christian Bible by the excision from the Old Testament of those books found in the Septuagint but not in the Hebrew Bible. The order of the Septuagint was retained to some extent (i.e. Daniel remained among the prophets), but the Hebrew Bible order was followed in the Book of the Twelve (prophets). In a sense the reformers went back to Jerome and followed his recommendations about the Hebrew canon. So they combined a Jewish-determined volume with a Christian-determined volume to produce a hybrid Bible – and rid themselves of a few minor warrants for Catholic beliefs into the bargain.

By the time the reformers appeared there had also developed a rediscovery of the Hebrew scriptures, so that Christian theologians were able to take instruction in Hebrew from Jewish teachers. This development contributed greatly to new translations of the Bible which by-passed the Vulgate and sought to produce more accurate translations and editions of the scriptures (the Catholic Erasmus was an outstanding example of this new learning). One important innovation of the reforming movements among the Christian churches was the central role given to the Bible in Christian belief and practice. Before the Reformation, tradition and ecclesiastical practice had been at least as important as holy scripture, and with the Renaissance reason had begun to make its presence felt in matters theological. But with the reformers the authoritarian structures of the Church were replaced by the authority of scripture, and the Church's magisterium gave way to the development of biblical hermeneutics. By the eighteenth century the scholasticism of biblical interpreters had more than equalled the medieval scholasticism of the Catholic Church, and the Bible had become as tyrannical an object as ever the Pope had been. However, such negative developments could hardly have been foreseen during the upheavals of the sixteenth century. Once the religious face of northern Europe had been changed from Catholic to Protestant (I generalize here) the Christian Bible had become available in two distinctive versions.

So since the sixteenth century it has been necessary to make a number of distinctions with reference to the Bible. Generalized references to the Bible *per se* have become fairly meaningless. The important first question is, 'which Bible?'. Or, to express that interrogative sentence in a slightly different form: 'Madam, are you Jewish, Catholic or Protestant?'. Where, for reasons of ecumenicity, members of different discourse modes meet to discuss the Bible, a certain amount of confusion is very likely to arise. Although there exists a Common Bible in English (an ecumenical edition of the Revised Standard Version), it is liable to offend against the sensibilities of those who prefer their own English version (without apocryphal and pseudepigraphal additions if they are 'good Protestants'). As hermeneutic frameworks are fundamental to interpreting the Bible, such ecumenical gatherings are doomed to confusion or very plain fare indeed. That is inevitable, because the Bible divides communities as much as it may unite some members of a particular religious community.

The reference to the books of the Bible in Ezra Pound's *Cantos* which forms the epigraph to this chapter reflects an extended use of the lines beyond their author's meaning. In the Pound quotation, naming the books of the Bible is a challenge to demonstrate genuine knowledge of the Bible, whereas in the argument I have been developing thus far such a naming of the books (assuming a high level of literacy in modern society) would indicate the religious affiliation of the speaker. For the books named would be different depending on

20

the speaker's commitment (Jew, Catholic or Protestant) and so the question 'wot are the books ov the bible?' functions as a way of detecting shibboleths. (A shibboleth, a fine biblical notion (see Judg. 12.1-6), is a use of language which betrays membership of a class of people. It is therefore an appropriate word to describe the phenomenon of commitment to different Bibles which distinguishes different groups of people.) Of course, with the exception of certain fundamentalist groups, the Bible is only a small part of any religious community's stock in trade, and so beliefs about the Bible should not be over-exaggerated. If at times churches of the Reformed persuasion give the impression of overvaluing the Bible and overemphasizing parts of it, that is probably due to unbalanced elements within those communities (see Chapter Three). The Bible *is* important for Jewish and Christian communities – whatever version is used – but it is far from being all-important. However, as I am writing a book about the Bible and its problematic nature and status in religious communities, this exclusive focus on the Bible rather than on communal beliefs and practices is inevitable.

The growth of critical method

This broad brush-stroke approach to the history of the development of the Bibles of various religious communities has omitted one significant group from its account. In the centuries after the Renaissance, European society was transformed by the scientific revolution, the age of Reason and the Enlightenment. The rise of rationalism saw also the emergence of new movements in theology and the study of the Bible, which helped to create modern critical theology and the historical-critical study of the Bible. From the vantage point of today it is possible to read the Bible in a critical way far removed from ancient dogmatic principles, and thereby to overcome the divisions of different Bibles and obligatory commitment to specific religious confessions. Critical theology has transformed the ways in which the Bible can be read and has helped to free human thought from worldviews constructed from a mixture of ancient philosophy and biblical imagery. Developed over centuries, the historical-critical study of the Bible (the version does not matter because the methodology is adequate to whatever Bible is used) allows the biblical literature to be read in the context of the time of its production rather than in accordance with the dictates of later dogmatic systems of belief. Eschewing religious dogma in favour of a rational approach to ancient literature, the critical study of the Bible allowed the book to be freed from many distorting influences, as well as freeing its readers from any tendency to idolize the book. Of course I am oversimplifying and idealizing a complex set of processes developed over the past four centuries, but at the centre of critical theology and the critical study of the Bible is a most welcome emancipatory movement away from post-Reformation tendencies to idolize the Word (an equivocal word when used of the Bible) and its concomitant tyranny over religious communities.

The struggle over the Bible which dominated Protestant circles in the nineteenth century, especially in the seminaries and universities, was eventually won by the critical approach, so that today academic theology is unimaginable without a commitment to the critical perspective. Like all ideological conflicts this victory was not won without serious losses, and heresy trials marked various stages in the robust resistance to allowing modern thought to gain a foothold in theological circles. But critical theory did not sweep away all opposition to the modern understanding of theology and the Bible. Rather, a kind of parallel world developed in which institutions devoted themselves to the pre-Copernican approach to the Bible, while the academy pursued the methods appropriate to a historical understanding of such literature. Again I oversimplify, because an acute analysis of the complexities of the struggles of the past two centuries would justify a book-length treatment itself. Many individuals in different institutions struggled to combine a critical approach to theology and the Bible with a devoted commitment to traditional forms of religion. The extent to which this hybrid form of life can be successfully sustained for any length of time is a matter for debate, and religious denominations today are often the site of fierce struggles between what may be described loosely as 'conservative' and 'radical' elements. There is in the larger intellectual world of scholarship and piety (the two are far from being opposed commitments) a complex gradation of allegiances.

On the one hand there is the community of scholars and on the other the community of believers. But many members of the latter community would also claim membership of the community of scholars, while many scholars would deny any connection with the community of believers. These then are overlapping communities.

In most academic enterprises there is no necessary conflict between the two, but there are subtle distinctions and evaluations which a Martian visitor might easily detect, though they are very difficult to articulate or map. There are also occasions and issues which do separate the two communities and force the theologians to acknowledge the priority of their belief commitment. A good example of where the dividing line can regularly be drawn is in the evaluation of the superiority of the Bible over other ancient literature, or in the tendency to denigrate other ancient religions (or their gods) in favour of what is reckoned to be the splendid virtues of biblical religion. In these evaluations, those who are solely members of the community of scholars are less likely to give way to such chauvinistic judgements. The true scholar reads accounts of the deeds of the gods, whether they be the actions of Marduk or Inanna, Amon or Isis, Yahweh or Anat, without yielding to the temptation to differentiate between these gods in favour of one of them. The matter is more complex than this example suggests, but it remains a good starting-point for a discussion of complicated issues.

Freed from the necessity of reading the Bible in servitude to *later* religious dogmas, the critical study of the Bible enables the reader to approach the collection of various books constituting the Bible (Jewish, Christian or Protestant), not to mention the much larger background literature from which the Bible came, as if it were a body of literary work like any other literature. Here we approach an interesting area of literary categorization which demands careful formulation. In a very real sense the Bible is unique. What makes it unique – as opposed to the truism that every book is unique in its own particularity – is the fact that there really is nothing like it in the history of literature. The Indian epic *Mahabharata* may be longer and older but it is all of a piece in that it tells a unified story. Whereas the Bible consists of a selection of books, in various languages and from many different provenances, written over many centuries and fused together (in various canons) in circumstances beyond our knowledge. Something comparable to the Bible, in English literature, would be a bound volume of selected books from Beowulf to Dickens, with a few Gaelic volumes thrown in for good measure. Some of the individual books in the Bible are very distinctive (e.g. gospels); and others, while generically similar to comparative literature of the period, have a particular quality to them which makes them outstanding examples of their genre (e.g. Job and some of Paul's letters). And yet the books of the Bible are so very much part and parcel of the ancient world which produced them. The one Moabite inscription which we possess reads uncannily like a page from the Hebrew Bible. Characters such as Saul and Job approximate to the creations of the Greek tragedians, and a line of Qoheleth is the equivalent of a Heraclitean fragment. Unique as a collection, yet tantalizingly similar in its parts to the literatures of its neighbouring cultures, what gives the Bible its edge in Western civilization is its formative contributions to the development of modern European culture. Here it has its equivalents in other cultures – the Qu'ran in Islam, the Rig-Veda and Bhagavad-Gita in India, Homer in ancient Greece.

Modern perspectives on the Bible have been determined by the critical enterprise. In pre-critical views of the Bible it was in popular regard (still is in many religious circles) in many ways a book of magic; wonderfully unique and divinely inspired, it was credited with great powers and held in awe as completely lacking in error of any kind. The critical reading of the Bible has exposed its errors and mistakes, its contradictions and contrarieties, its xenophobic values and its many advocacies of violence, intolerance and hatred of others. At the same time the critical approach to the Bible has released its great literary and aesthetic qualities from the ecclesiastical captivity of the book. The Hebrew Bible has been freed from the christological manacles imposed on it in Christian circles, and has had restored to it its own integrity as a collection of books independent of Christian functionalism. Now, Jews and Christians can read the Hebrew Bible together without Christian imperialism determining the hermeneutic modes of reading. Biblical scholars may be Jewish, Christian (of any denominational allegiance), agnostic or atheist, and share a common discipline with common goals. The critical study of the Bible (Hebrew, Greek or New Testament) has broken down the wall between Jews, Christians and others *as scholars*. In matters ecclesiastical the divisions remain the same, and the various versions of the Bible separate different communities, in conjunction with other religious beliefs and commitments. I do not wish to gloss over the ideological quarrels of scholars or to suggest that the academy is a wonderfully eirenic centre of pure study (it is not), but the truth of the matter stated in this paragraph is undeniable as a principle underlying the critical study of the Bible. The critical enterprise is a commonalty shared in by all scholars who embrace the methodology and values of that study.

The transformations of biblical study which the critical method has developed over the past few centuries are too many to enumerate here, but one is worth mentioning by way of example. The older dogmatic Christian reading of the biblical prophets understood them in a christological fashion. Such prophets were seen as predictors of the future in the very specific sense of a messianic future where Jesus was the Messiah. Much of the New Testament is incomprehensible without this firm belief about the prophets. In many ways the New Testament writers ransacked the Greek Bible for predictions to apply to Jesus or for quotations which could ornament their accounts of his life and work. The modern critical reading of the prophets minimizes the predictive element in their writings, because the dominant features to be found in them when they are read in a historical way do not include messianic predictions about the future. Seen in their own time, the prophets cease being ventriloquists' dummies and become very much part of a complex social movement of struggle about values and practice. They are no longer colonized by the New Testament and converted into Christians *avant la lettre*, but have their historical integrity restored to them.

In the same way the Hebrew Bible ceases to be a prologue to the New Testament, as if the continued existence of Jews and the emergence of Judaism after the rise of Christian communities had never happened. It becomes (the context of my remarks here is European culture, for of course among Jews the book always had its integrity and the prophets never were foretellers of Jesus) a collection of books in its own right and not a quarry for Christian furnishings. Again I must not pretend that this ideal description of the critical method produced an idyllic relation between Jews and Christians. Far from it. In fact the accusation has been made against nineteenth-century critical scholarship that much of its German manifestation was thoroughly anti-semitic. This accusation describes social background and prevailing political ideological factors in German scholarship, not to mention the fact that in that century most biblical scholars were Christian by persuasion. But the social context of scholarship is a very complex matter and is beyond my brief here.

Restoring the historical dimension to the biblical prophets did not entail making the New Testament use of the prophets nonsensical or incomprehensible. It did however produce a distinction between the author's meaning of a text (or its historical sense) and the subsequent uses made of that text by other writers. Here the study of the Bible in terms of the meaning of the text (the historical meaning) shades into the study of the interpretation of the Bible throughout history. The history of the interpretation of the Bible (the technical German term for this is *Rezeptionsgeschichte* 'the history of the reception' of the text) is a colossal field of study and one which is beyond the capabilities of the individual scholar to master in its entirety. As part of the reception of the Hebrew/Greek Bible, the New Testament handling of the prophets may be regarded as a particular *use* of them or an interpretation of them following a Christian hermeneutic. Such a hermeneutic would transform the meaning of a text so that it served the purposes of writers in a very different social context. In the light of the new hermeneutic, old texts would take on a new meaning, would come to life in a different way. Thus the emergent Christian communities read selected texts from the past and transformed them into their present. What the critical study of the Bible does is to restore the pastness of such texts and attempt to reconstruct the conditions under which the original texts were produced.

It is not difficult to see why traditional Christian modes of reading what was called the *Old* Testament (a controlling title which asserted the obsolescence of the Jewish scriptures except as prologue to the Christian story) should be at loggerheads with the critical study of the Bible. The critical method has virtually unravelled the whole of Christian history by asserting the integrity of the Hebrew Bible as a book independent of Christian structures. If the critical reading of the Bible had any force then it rendered the Christian Bible problematic for Christians. This was a devastating blow, especially for Protestant upholders of traditional biblical interpretation. Although most branches of Protestantism have made an uneasy peace with the critical study of the Bible and the larger denominations have embraced it in their teaching institutions, opposition to critical theology and biblical criticism remains endemic among the churches and is one of the main shibboleths of those movements which journalists loosely call 'fundamentalist'. In the twentieth century, critical theology also made inroads into Catholic thought, and the critical study of the Bible now also flourishes in many of the teaching institutions of the Catholic Church. Needless to say there is also much opposition to it, and that Church still has a sufficiently authoritarian structure to be able to impose sanctions on teachers who appear to stray too far from the paths of orthodox thought.

Critical method and belief

The modern competent reader will have no difficulty in discovering why the Bible is problematic for theology or for certain beliefs about the Bible. A serious reading of the Bible, with or without benefit of the critical method, will reveal many mismatches between what is in the book and what is believed about the book. This is natural and inevitable, because a large-scale untidy collection of books such as constitutes the Bible (the version is immaterial) could not be expected to tally with later systems of thought developed under circumstances alien to the Bible (see Chapter Two). The high degree of selectivity required to carve out of the Bible an adequately consistent set of biblical images and notions (a selectivity which inevitably leaves a residue of unused material larger than the set chosen) must make the conscientious reader pause for serious thought. Books which contain contradictions and contrarieties make either impossible or highly ludicrous the production of consistent, coherent beliefs derived from them. This is not only because contradiction and opposing metaphors make consistency and coherence impossible to attain, but it is also due to the nature of the biblical language. A book so dominated by poetic imagery as the Bible is, and made up of writings from many different hands, cannot yield a system of thought without readers doing serious affront to its linguistic integrity. A series of metaphoric images will produce various word-pictures of different possibilities rather than fixed dogmas of belief. The selection of certain preferred images over other possible images yields at best one picture among many; it does not constitute an exhaustive account of biblical language. Formal contradictions within the historical books will militate against certain traditional claims made about the Bible.

Perhaps the most important area of biblical studies for observing the devastating effects of the critical approach has been the New Testament Gospels and the representation of the figure of Jesus. While many Christians may have found it possible to tolerate mistakes and contradictions, moral problems and untoward behaviour, in the books they regarded as the Old Testament, the exposure of the Gospels to criticism posed very serious problems for them. The traditional harmonizing of the Gospels had allowed most people

27

to imagine that the four Gospels were, in some sense, reliable eye-witness accounts of the life and death of Jesus. Biblical criticism changed all that. Now it is impossible to read the Gospels without recognizing the important roles played by the (unknown) writers who finally produced them. The different and often conflicting representations of Jesus in the canonical Gospels have to be taken into account when making statements about what Jesus might or might not have said or done. A wise reader of the Gospels will cautiously talk about 'the Jesus of Mark' or 'the Jesus of the Fourth Gospel', without making the mistake of thinking or implying that the *historical* Jesus actually did or said such things. The historical Jesus has become profoundly problematical, and much orthodox Christian theology feels itself to be undermined by such developments. This is certainly one of the most important sites of struggle in contemporary theological and ecclesiastical circles, because if the Jesus of the New Testament Gospels is as much (if not more) the product of human fancy and storytelling as he is of reliable historical reportage, then certain religious dogmas are felt to be seriously undermined. Again my simple sweep of two thousand years of thought takes me into deep waters which are uncharted for the purposes of this book, so I must withdraw from an area which would warrant many books rather than a few brief sentences. What must be acknowledged, however, is the fact that belief in the historical Jesus cannot survive the critical enterprise *unchanged*. It must come to terms with and adopt some of the findings of critical biblical study or retreat completely into traditional dogmas imposed on the text. In this sense biblical criticism has triumphed over all alternative approaches. It has imposed its terms on the debate and shaped the methodological considerations which determine the discussion.

It is important to remember that the critical study of the Bible is a method rather than a fixed set of findings. The results of the application of the method may vary from researcher to researcher, so that modern biblical criticism covers a wide range of different opinions on how the Bible should be read. This means that the individual scholar may be both a biblical critic and the most devout of practising Jews or Christians. Religious devotion not being determined by the Bible or any particular method of reading it, there is no necessary connection between commitment to a specific religious way of life and the holding of the most critical views on the Bible. Most scholars are probably fairly devout people because, the universities apart, the institutions which study the Bible tend to have church or denominational associations. Religious faith may include beliefs about the Bible or have values associated with the Bible, but generally its determinative factors are governed by a number of important beliefs relatively independent of the Bible. Belief in the existence of God, beliefs about the nature of that God, commitment to a specific church tradition and membership of a particular worshipping community, are all fundamental matters shaping how and why people believe. In Protestant circles the Bible may play a large part in some of these matters, but most biblical scholars happily commit themselves to active church life without any diminution of their Christian commitment (*mutatis mutandis* the same may be said of Jewish biblical scholars). So the critical study of the Bible is in no sense incompatible with religious commitment. It is of course in serious opposition to many traditional beliefs *about* the Bible, and incompatible with worldviews derived from the Bible.

The critical study of the Bible, being fundamentally a modern approach to the ancient books, shares with other post-Enlightenment movements a worldview which is determined by modern scientific thought. No critical scholar believes that Genesis 1—3 affords scientific information about how the earth or humankind came into existence. As poetry or myth this passage may have high value for religious or imaginative people, but it is worthless as a series of statements about cosmology or anthropology. The scientific or critical viewpoint is determined by the latest state of knowledge and is always corrigible. Dogma and religious belief are determined by other factors and are generally regarded as incorrigible. Whether religion and science are fundamentally incompatible because they reflect entirely discrete (i.e. mutually exclusive) worldviews has been debated for centuries, but many scientists have resolved any conflict between the two by practising both. Often that means reducing Genesis 1—3 to the equivalent of 'there is a God who created the universe' and then treating the rest of the material as poetic myth. What survives the transformation is the metaphor of human beings 'made in the divine image', which is then given an absolute status in any subsequent theological construction put on the reinterpreted Genesis stories. Such a marriage of science and religion usually rationalizes the Bible at those points where no modern thinker could conceivably take the biblical imagery literally.

How individual scholars may reconcile a modern scientific

approach to the world with as traditional a reading of the Bible as they feel they can sustain is a matter of psychology as well perhaps as of church politics. In some cases the conflict between the two possibilities illustrates well the sense in which the Bible is problematic for Christianity today. There is of course no absolute necessity for any theologian or scholar to adhere to any traditional view or interpretation of the Bible. It can now be read as one would read any collection of literature from the past, with due allowance for the problems of understanding such material and due acknowledgement of the role it has played in Western civilization. It does not seem to me that the ancient dogma of biblical inspiration has any more significance now for the study of the Bible than other outmoded beliefs of the medieval worldview. (I know that the dogma is felt to be very important in many religious circles, but these are precisely the areas where the medieval worldview continues to prevail in matters of religion.) The critical study of the Bible belongs to the modern world, and like all modern worldviews has displaced previous viewpoints. It is not possible to hold to the medieval Ptolemaic view of cosmology and accept a modern cosmological account of the universe as well. Traditional views about the Bible were derived from the metaphysics of ancient thought and so the change of paradigm entailed by the loss of medieval metaphysics and the development of the modern scientific viewpoint inevitably means the abandonment of such views.

The continued treatment in the West of the Bible as an important collection of very diverse writings and as a significant cultural object, means that the radical changes in the way it is viewed and read are indicative of changing modes of discourse. Still important for cultural and intellectual (i.e. literary and historical) reasons, the Bible is no longer an authoritative source of information on the world in which we live. It remains one historical source of material which has helped to shape the way social structures have come to be, and for many religious people it is still regarded as an important guide to ethics and values. The critical approach does not necessarily rule out such uses of the Bible, though it invariably entails serious modification of how it should be used where prescriptive interpretations are involved. Certain modes of discourse – literary, cultural, poetic and religious – still use the Bible (with other important literary materials), but always in conjunction with thoroughly modern approaches to it. Old-fashioned religious communities will go on using the Bible in ancient ways because many of these function as refuges from modernity as well as also being places where sophisticated modern people (e.g. scientists, doctors of medicine) can be naïve in matters religious. As a reservoir of images and a repository of metaphors the Bible will continue as a cultural factor in educated, literate circles – evidence of this role is amply to be seen in the recent phenomenon of 'the Bible as/and literature' courses in the universities and publishing houses of the West. Of course the steady decrease in literacy in Western civilization will make inroads into the aesthetic appreciation of the Bible as literature, and if 'fundamentalism', with its distaste for considering the Bible as 'literature', continues to thrive the Bible as cultural object will become ever more despised.

A critical study of the Bible cannot diminish the role it has played in the development of European and American literature. Atheist or Pope will have to know the book of Jonah to appreciate fully the roots and greatness of Herman Melville's novel *Moby Dick*. Stefan Heym's novel *The King David Report* is unimaginable without the biblical story of David and Solomon, as is Joseph Heller's *God Knows*. Thomas Mann's tetralogy *Joseph and His Brothers* is a magnificent retelling of the biblical story of Joseph – a story which is told in about fourteen pages in the Bible. The two novels by Melville and Mann are excellent examples of how the compactness of biblical narrative can be expanded from tales of brevity to astonishingly lengthy works. Between the two nodalities of biblical story and literary treatment stretches a complex intellectual world of immense significance which cannot be diminished by the critical reading of the Bible or enhanced by more 'fundamentalist' tendencies. Such a history of the reception of the Bible is more likely to flourish under the governance of the critical method than under more pious methods which constrain the biblical text with dogmatic systems of thought derived from the non-biblical world. In the final analysis, then, it becomes a question of whether the Bible will fall among the Philistines or will survive on a critical level of reading with and without religious dimensions.

It is beyond the capacity of this writer in the space of a chapter to give an adequate account of the Bible itself (in whatever version) and its long history of reception. Two different things are involved here: a description of what the Bible contains in its various languages and translations, and an analysis of the beliefs about and interpretations of the various Bibles over the past two thousand years. In many religious communities it is assumed that repeating or paraphrasing what is to be found in parts of the Bible, somehow forms an exhaustive account of what may be said about the book. Paraphrasing the Bible explains nothing. It merely repeats what the text is imagined to say – though often under the assumption that a prescriptive code is in operation. In the modern world it is no longer possible to pretend that things have not changed radically or that the medieval worldview still holds sway over the minds and hearts of people. We must read the Bible to find out what it says, and so describe that as to produce an accurate account of what is in its various versions. That is only half the task. The other half is what the critical method is all about: the setting of that accurate account in its historical forms and period and the evaluation of it in terms of where we are now. Linguists and anthropologists use the terms 'emic' and 'etic' to describe these two approaches. Derived from the phonemic/ phonetic distinction, these are useful words for distinguishing between a viewpoint from inside the system itself (emic) and one from outside the system (etic). What seems to me to be profoundly misleading in modern religious thinking is the confusion of an imagined emic standpoint with a prescriptive account of the Bible.

Finally, it must be said that the critical study of the Bible only changes people who are prepared to be changed. The older modes of reading the Bible survive intact in some circles, and newer methods replace some of the older critical techniques in areas where people wish for a more positive reading of texts than they imagine the critical method can deliver. The two historical levels of traditional and critical can be transformed into a spectrum ranging from the critical mode at one end to the more normal religious treatment of the Bible as commodity and fetish. Between science and superstition there are fewer steps and more connections than people often imagine. The rise of the critical study of the Bible has not replaced or even displaced (except in the academies) more traditional uses and interpretations. Hence it is possible for people to continue to imagine the universe as if it reflected the cosmological dimensions of any of the various views of the world expressed in parts of the Bible. It is still possible for religious communities to make snake-handling the high point of their services on the basis of belief in the spurious ending of Mark's Gospel (16.9-20), or for individual pietists to hide Bibles under the seats at spiritualist meetings in order to frustrate the clairvoyant powers of the speakers. This is the silly end of the spectrum, and the critical method is not going to spoil anybody's sense of fun or treatment of the Bible as a fetish. On the other hand, the serious reader of the Bible in the modern world is going to find that book (in whatever version) a highly problematic volume. Just how problematic I hope to explore a little further in what follows.

2

God
the Hidden Problematic

. . . any religion which does not say that God is hidden is not true.

Blaise Pascal

In faith itself we are forced to say that our knowledge of God begins in all seriousness with the knowledge of the hiddenness of God . . .

Karl Barth

God is the problematic. In the most general and universal of senses this is true for all human beings and most human societies. The question of the existence of God has proved throughout human history to be inherently unanswerable, except in the context of religious communities, where membership implies an existential commitment to an affirmation of divine existence. Philosophers, theologians and thoughtful people have generally found it to be a question which eludes a provable answer, though there have been no end of quests to demonstrate the existence of God. The traditional proofs have not fared well in modern philosophical thought, and most people who believe in God do so for reasons somewhat beyond rational articulation. Religious philosophers continue to produce variations on the classical proofs, and do so in the service of different religious traditions. But even where they have shown to their own satisfaction that such a divine entity may be said to exist and also to conform to the specifications laid down by their own denominational or cultural religion, the most they have usually shown is that, under certain circumstances, it may not be unreasonable to believe in the proposition that a divine being exists. Change the circumstances, and the so-called demonstration evaporates like the morning mist. The existence of God remains problematic.

That is how it should be. For to be able to demonstrate the existence of God and also to show that this being conformed to human specifications as laid down by time-conditioned, culturally-shaped presuppositions (i.e. religious systems of thought) would be to have produced an idol or a monster. It would be a god in human image. If the definition of the divine is to include that which is beyond human comprehension, then any account of God which knows as much as traditional religions claim to know about such a being offends against that principle. Creeds and confessions, Bibles and Qu'rans, all appear to be able to specify the inside-leg measurements of their god to such a degree of accuracy that they can persecute and prosecute any who differ from them in any detail. Religious history is filled with the corpses of people who knew less about the god than the creeds and sacred books permitted, or who knew other than was asserted in such sources.

Lurking in many religions is an awareness that the idea (or reality) of God is something profoundly beyond human imagination. At a very real level of symbolic forms there is little difference between atheism and theism when it comes to making assertions about the mysterious ground of being, or about that which the human mind can neither grasp nor define. Both atheist and theist confess themselves to be baffled by the divine. The atheist denies signification to what is beyond the sayable and the theist relies on traditional beliefs to flesh out what cannot be said. I suspect that really intelligent people walk away from both positions and seek to live their lives as best they can in a universe without adequate resources for determining such recondite subjects as the existence (or otherwise) of a being beyond definition.

Within religious systems, devotees may assume the existence of God and busy themselves with the practicalities imposed by such a belief. Such practices have been constructed culturally over many centuries, and are perfectly adequate means of overcoming the deficiencies of the intellectual side of the believer's commitment. Without ever having to assert any problems with belief in the existence of God, from time to time even the most devout believers may allow a shadow of perplexity about divine dealings in the universe to cross their mind. They may just occasionally yield to the temptation to complain about the state of the universe, or give voice to vexed puzzlement at what they perceive to be an injustice inherent in the way things are. That fleeting moment of puzzled enquiry – addressed often to the deity – may be described in many ways; one of the more interesting biblical metaphors is that of divine hiding. The hidden God is one image which suggests an awareness among some of the biblical writers that belief in God was not necessarily an unproblematic matter. Hence any religious system which wished to derive some of its basic beliefs from the Bible might well find the problem to be inherent in any representation of the divine in the world. On the other hand, it might prefer to discard any notion of the hiddenness of God as being incompatible with dogmas of divine revelation and the concomitant certitude of believers in matters of 'revealed truth'.

Hebrew imagery and Greek thought

This tension between a biblical metaphor and a system of religious belief (e.g. the dogmatics of conciliar Christianity) is a very good illustration of what makes the Bible problematic for theology. Biblical language harnessed to the dogmatic constructions of Greek-inspired philosophical theology helped to produce some of the elements of early Christian beliefs. But biblical metaphors were taken over and translated into Hellenistic thought patterns, so that they were freighted with alien concepts. Hebrew imagery survived, but in Greek dress and transformed by the hermeneutics of the Septuagint translators and the later theologians who were steeped in Greek philosophy. In the emergence of the post-Constantine churches and the development of Christian orthodoxy, it was Greek substantive philosophy that created the main features of what became Christian dogmas. Thus the prophet Jesus of Nazareth, a perfectly good biblical model of social critic and messenger of the divine, became with time and theological reflection the second person of a divine trinity. Hellenistic circles of Jewish thought may have contributed to that kind of linguistic thinking, but Greek substantive philosophy was the discourse mode which determined the dogmas of the creeds. Communities which followed the teachings of Jesus within a Jewish context became with time less and less able to compete against the imperial sponsorship of the emergent orthodox churches, and eventually disappeared from history (or were disappeared, to use a contemporary term from the critique of political power structures).

The mismatch between biblical metaphor and dogmatic theology is perhaps more apparent to the modern observer of ecclesiastical history (because of the vantage point provided by critical theology) than it might have been to those who controlled the development of how the ancient writings were handled in the production of such dogmatic theology. Theology operates with abstract philosophical notions, whereas much of the language of the Bible is highly metaphorical. In philosophical talk, God is abstract; ontological categories govern this prime mover. In biblical language, God is a character in a narrative, a player in a story. The existence of God is assumed. It is never argued for, because the Hebrew Bible comes out of a pre-philosophical world. God is taken for granted by the biblical writers, and the communities in which these writers lived were committed to belief in God (or at least gods). So while the philosophical mind seeks to argue for the existence of a divine being, argument is redundant in a context determined by biblical language. Jewish and early Christian arguments about the existence of the divine being were done in the context of competing theologies rather than as philosophical arguments. All groups believed in divine beings; the questions which divided them had more to do with shape and size than with existence. The biblical writers, having their roots in polytheistic cultures, could assume many things about the divine and use different descriptions of that being without needing to have recourse to consistent or systematic considerations. The notion of systematic thought comes from Greek philosophy and is not to be found in the Hebrew Bible. That is one of the big reasons why the Bible is problematic for theology.

The God depicted throughout the Hebrew Bible is very much an Oriental potentate. Immensely powerful, generally all-knowing and much given to outbursts of temper, this being manipulates humans and regularly intervenes in situations in order to achieve certain ends. If every description and depiction of the biblical God, whose names are legion (Yahweh, Elohim, El, Eloah, Shaddai, Yahweh Elohim, etc.), were taken together they would not add up to a single, consistent description but would produce a series of conflicting, and conceivably contradictory, images of the divine. Metaphor and image are more difficult to relate to contradiction than statements and propositions, so biblical language is less damaged than philosophical theology by contradictions and contrarieties. But if that language is to be roped into the service of theology then its conflicting images will become problematic. For images in conflict cannot produce a consistent theology. Theology, with its philosophical parentage of consistency and coherence, is very vulnerable to the shifting sands of biblical metaphor. God may be a philosophically or theologically coherent rational notion, but the God of the Bible is not. Such a being was never constructed from philosophical thought, so cannot be expected to conform to the norms of systematic abstract thought. What contributed to the representation of God in the Bible were many discrete and diverse streams of thought, reflection and highly imaginative language. The multivariant sources and traditions behind the biblical writings could not be expected to have produced a consistent or simple account of the deity; so too much should not be made of the inconsistencies.

Biblical language (Hebrew or Greek) constitutes a web of poetic metaphors and a network of significant narratives (significance here being determined by the redactors of the final collections) and such things have to be judged by literary, aesthetic and cultural criteria rather than philosophical and theological standards. The biblical God is a character in Hebrew narrative and therefore is, in a very real sense, a figure of fiction. This fictional character is regularly named Yahweh (the conventional vocalization of the tetragrammaton YHWH; in a previous age the favoured vocalization of it yielded Jehovah) and can be observed behaving in many humanlike ways. Thus Yahweh goes down to the city of Babel in the plain of Shinar during the construction of the city in order to see the city and in particular its (famous?) tower (Genesis 11.1-6). Then he and his companions (the force of the verbs in verse 7) go down in order to confuse the language of the builders and he scatters them across the face of the earth. Elements of the human and the divine are mixed in that representation of Yahweh. Other gods or divine beings of some kind (however shadowy) are his colleagues, though their contribution to the stories is fairly limited (cf. Genesis 1.26; 6.1-4; 18.1-22). They constitute a dialogical context for Yahweh and may be a fictional device for externalizing the deity's thoughts. The polytheistic roots of the stories are clear, but the biblical writers have the idiom under control and use it to develop their storytelling (only Genesis 6.1-4 is seriously problematic). In Job 1—2 one of those companions catches the deity out in a moment of hubris and wreaks untold havoc on Job and his family as a result of that all-too-human lapse on the part of Yahweh. The exchanges between Yahweh and the Satan (adversary) in those framing chapters of the book of Job indicate a character somewhat prone to vanity and not above wagering other people's lives to settle a dispute with one of his servants.

Many other biblical stories could be used as examples of Yahweh as a character in the fictional modes of the Hebrew writers. But multiplying examples will not make the point any better than the illustrations already used. Narratological techniques used by the writers of the Bible represent a deity who is a character in many of the stories, even though he (that gender marker is an inevitable feature of the Bible) may often be the most powerful of figures. Where necessary Yahweh is always in control, though in some stories he may function as one element among others. Thus in the story of Micaiah ben Imlah's vision (1 Kings 22) Yahweh is represented as sitting on his throne between the host of heaven (other divine beings) and debating the matter of how to trap king Ahab into his death. As in the Job story Yahweh goes along with a particular course of action, even though it offends against all ethical principles. Being the source of power, deities are not usually entirely subjected to the ethical norms of the community. Whatever the relationship between Yahweh and his companions, he does appear to be rather prone to letting their schemes loose on the earth. In this sense he is really no different from the Homeric Zeus or the gods of any of the ancient Near Eastern cultures. The gods can be merciless in their dealings with humans, and exceptionally cruel. The fictional character of Yahweh is no better: the story of the young Samuel is told in equally cruel terms (1 Samuel 2.27—3.18). Mantic voices speak out against the house of Eli: an anonymous figure predicts a horrific future for his family. Then the young Samuel is visited by Yahweh and told a tale designed to make the ears tingle. When Samuel reveals all to Eli the old priest is able to recognize the character behind such cruel tales. His response, 'It is Yahweh,' reflects an all too painful acknowledgement of that force which kills and brings to life (1 Samuel 2.6). Similar representations of Yahweh in the prophetic books identify his actions with the vicious invasions of the Assyrians and the Babylonians. Nebuchadrezzar, the butcher of Babylon, is Yahweh's servant and has Jerusalem razed to the ground. The cruel Assyrians are his instrument of wrath. In a savage world the power behind the savagery is Yahweh.

As tales go, these depictions of a cruel god slaughtering thousands of people are standard accounts to be found in the literatures of all ancient cultures. There is nothing exceptional about them except for the fact that in post-biblical times they were incorporated into the sacred writings of a very powerful social force which spread across Europe to become Christendom. By the time Christendom had been established, the theological superstructure of emergent Catholic Christianity had been created by the councils, creeds and teaching institutions of the churches. In this dogmatic network the definition of God had become trinitarian and theologically highly abstract, so that the biblical stories came to be read as if there were a simple equation between the fictional mode of representing Yahweh and the unmoved mover behind the universe. Yahweh, the character in many a stirring tale, became the eternal One without body, parts or passions. There is the heart of the problem constituted by the Bible for Christianity.

Let me spell this point out for all those readers of the Bible who would claim to see no problem at all between an abstract theological system of belief and a congeries of concrete narratological images. In stories a character may behave in many different ways, and the only limits on behaviour are those inherent in the character as represented or as determined by the conditions prevailing in the story being told. A collection of different stories from a variety of sources using the same or similar characters would be under no necessity to have a consistent representation of that character. There would, no doubt, be family resemblances between most, if not all, the stories, but the character would not have to conform to what we would understand as the laws of contradiction. A character in fiction may behave in a contradictory fashion in ways not allowed to real people or not expected in philosophical argument. Aristotelian logic is not a regulative principle of fictional representation. However, if the equation is made between the biblical representation of Yahweh and the God of the creeds of theology, then major problems arise. It is the theological appropriation of the Bible, or, alternatively, the invasion of religion by philosophy (which produces theology in the first place), which constitutes the problem, and which makes the Bible such an uneasy object in the temple of theology. Produced by forces quite distinct from the urge to philosophize, the Bible is not at home in the theologizing of the philosophical. The philosophical demand for argument that is both consistent and coherent is a harsh standard to impose on tales told from cultures and times not party to Greek philosophical discourse.

In other words, the problem of the Bible for theology is in the first instance the presence of contradictions in the Bible. Not discrepancies of account or contradictions in narratives about historical events – the Bible has many of these – but contradictions in the representation of God. Theology is about God, so a source for doing theology which contains contradictions is invariably problematic. Discourse about God cannot tolerate formal contradictions. A philosophical system which was content to entertain such contradictions would itself be seen as a contradiction in terms (an oxymoron).

Contradictions in 1 Samuel 15

A few examples of such biblical contradictions will suffice to illustrate the problem – the multiplication of examples will not make the point any truer. In 1 Samuel 15 the long-running hostilities between king Saul and the prophet Samuel come to a head. Having annihilated the Amalekites (v.7), with the exception of Agag the Amalekite king and some of the best booty, Saul is confronted by a Samuel who recounts to him the divine word he had heard. The divine word is stated to have been the oracular 'I repent that I have made Saul king; for he has turned back from following me, and has not performed my commandments' (v.11), but Samuel says much more to Saul (vv. 16–23). In a series of dialogical exchanges between prophet and king, Samuel finally adds a statement of divine principle to his arguments. 'And also the Glory of Israel will not lie or repent; for he is not human that he should repent' (v. 29). In so far as any theology can be extracted from such a tale it must be the statement in verse 29. Yahweh (assuming that the epithetic 'glory of Israel' is equivalent to the divine name) is not human so he does not repent (i.e. change his mind) or lie. Human beings may change their minds or lie but Israel's God is not of that ilk. The statement would be uncontentious were it not for the fact that what is said in verse 11 plainly contradicts verse 29!

Whatever meaning may be attached to the word 'repent' (the same Hebrew word *niham* is used throughout the story) in the clash between Saul and Samuel, there is no escaping the problem which verse 29 poses for the theological interpretation of the divine

character. As the Hebrew Bible has many similar statements about
the deity repenting of actions and intentions (e.g. Gen. 6.6; cf. 1 Sam.
2.30; Jonah 3.9–10), the claim that he does not repent because he is
not human is the problematic element in the Samuel story. If there is
anything remotely resembling a dogma about Yahweh in the Bible it
must be the viewpoint that Yahweh repents (Jer. 18.7–10; the story
of Jonah), so a categorical denial of divine repentance is a statement
that inevitably strikes the reader of 1 Samuel 15 as odd. A book which
contains such an assertion in the context of its counter-assertion is a
philosopher's nightmare and ought to give theologians pause for
serious reflection. Either Yahweh repents (as humans do) or Yahweh
does not repent (unlike humans). Both cannot be true. That, in Western
logic, is the law of the excluded middle. It is also a violation of the rules
about contradiction. So if theological systems are to be founded on the
Bible they are going to run into serious problems in 1 Samuel 15.

Stumbling over contradictions in literature is no way to read
properly or to take texts seriously. Focusing on specific contradictions
does not assist one's appreciation of a story, so I must emphasize the
point that my only interest in the contradiction of 1 Samuel 15.29 is in
the context of demonstrating the unsuitability of the Bible for the
creation of theological dogmas. Dogmatic systems which attempt to
colonize the Bible are treating the book with contempt and forcing it
into a Procrustean bed. The more serious theological problem is of
course the oft-repeated claim that Yahweh repents, because a deity
who regularly changes his mind cannot be equated with the Eternal
unmoved mover. As a character in a book of tales, Yahweh is fully
entitled to chop and change according to plot and characterization;
but between that character and the Spirit behind the universe there is
a considerable gap. It is not possible to make any equation between
the Yahweh of the biblical narratives and the God of the creeds and
confessions of the churches, even though clever theologians may be
able to adjust the gap between the two so that it is narrower under
certain conditions. The Bible will remain problematic for theology.

1 Samuel 15 – a critical reading

Before developing the argument further it may be worth returning to
1 Samuel 15 in order to make a few observations on how the formal
contradiction in the text might be dealt with by a critical reading. The

critical approach lacks a straitjacket of dogmatic control, and so can approach texts open to the possibility of contradiction. Contextualizing verse 29 in the story of how Yahweh repented of having made Saul king, one explanation of the problem would be to see an ironic element at work in the final production of the text. Having noted that sometimes Yahweh does go back on his promises and, like humans, repents of his intentions (who could doubt this after working through 1 Samuel 2—3 and 13.1–15 to reach chapter 15?) the final writer (assuming more than one hand produced the story in its entirety) wanted to make the point that Yahweh might have repented of having made Saul king but he was certainly not going to repent of that repentance. Verse 29 might have started life as a marginal note on verse 28, or as the beginning of an attempt to modify or control the waywardness of Yahweh's predilection for repenting. The verse is so stark in the context of its present location that it is difficult to imagine that the original writer would not have been aware of its contradictory nature in the first place.I do not wish to subscribe to the theory of what has often been lampooned as the 'brainless redactor' (or a very large family of brainless redactors) who apparently put the Bible together as we know it, so I must wonder why verse 29 appears in the story. Why make a point which is contradicted by the whole story? Perhaps as a marginal note which has found its way into our text it represents a theologizing voice (who can guess the tone?) intent on pinning down Saul's dismissal: 'Of this one thing you can be sure – Yahweh does not repent of repenting about Saul.' The grandiose specifications of the verse suggest an attempt to formulate a principle. The principle may sit uneasily in this particular story, but some reader of the tale of the star-crossed leader of ancient Israel responded to the story with enough passion to make the assertion about the stuff Yahweh is made of. The verse does tend to deconstruct the story and undermine the principle of Yahweh's repentance. It certainly disrupts the reader in search of systematic principles gleaned from the biblical text to shore up a dogmatic system of theology imagined to be dependent on the Bible.

Divine deception

Among the elementary truths of theology might be imagined to be the claim that the gods do not tell lies. If the gods lie, then we are all in trouble because we will never be able to be certain about anything connected with our religious foundations. (Descartes faced a similar problem about whether the deity could have deceived us and thereby undermined his philosophical foundations.) 'God is truth' is a foundational claim of every religious system and a certitude embraced by every member of a theological community. What makes the Bible so problematic for theology is the representation in some of its narratives of Yahweh as a being who uses lies or encourages deception in order to get his own way. The counter-assertion has already been encountered in 1 Samuel 15.29 where it is stated that Israel's glory does not lie. But in the story of Micaiah ben Imlah's vision referred to earlier in this chapter there is a prime example of Yahweh's involvement with lies. The problem represented by Micaiah's account of the divine throne-room is a logistical one in which Yahweh is seeking an effective strategy for enticing Ahab to his death (1 Kings 22.19–23). Yahweh's problem is resolved by a spirit who volunteers to be 'a lying spirit in the mouth of all his prophets' (v. 22). Yahweh commands the spirit to go forth and entice Ahab and promises success. I suppose a desperate theologian might want to make subtle distinctions between encouraging others to lie and lying oneself, but both practices seem to be on the wrong side of truth-telling.

The divine deception of kings and prophets is a minor motif running through the biblical narratives about prophets. Deception comes from Yahweh (e.g. Ezek. 14.9; Jer. 4.10) because where prophets are involved divine inspiration is inevitably a part of the story, and if prophets speak the words of Yahweh it must be assumed that deception is always a possibility. No one can distinguish between words spoken under the influence of Yahweh and words spoken out of a prophet's own mind. If the two activities could be differentiated the Hebrew Bible would not be so full of lengthy tirades against the prophets (e.g. Jer. 23.9–40; 27—29; Ezek. 13.1—14.9; Mic. 3.5–8). The claim to speak for the gods is easily made, but testing the truth of the claim has so far defeated the wit of human communities. If the deities also deceive human beings, then inspiration itself becomes part of the problem. Ignoring or silencing the prophet may be the community's only escape from deception.

All ancient religions and literatures have representations of gods deceiving humans or speaking falsely through prophets. In that sense the Bible is like all the other products of human communities. Its writers could describe the problem but could not control it. Later communities would set up rules (cf. Deut. 13.1-5; 18.15-22; the *Didache*), including even the production of canons of sacred scriptures, attempting to control the inspired voice, but all in vain. Regulating the prophets always runs the risk of silencing the god or embracing the false. But the problem goes deeper. If the god also is capable of deceiving the prophet then those who listen to prophets are vulnerable to being deceived. The representation by certain biblical writers of Yahweh as a deceiver of prophets, queers theology's pitch.

God as creator of evil

God as problematic in the Bible can be explored further. Changing mind, lying and deceiving are merely human qualities used in the characterization of Yahweh, one of the main characters in the biblical narratives. They are negative features which may be balanced by the more positive qualities of divine passion and love. But what makes a god God is power, especially the power to create. As creator, Yahweh is presented as the one responsible for the production of the universe. All gods play this role of creator. But in ascribing creative powers to Yahweh the Hebrew Bible also acknowledges that Yahweh *created* evil. Second Isaiah represents Yahweh as saying: 'I am Yahweh and there is no other, forming light and creating darkness, making *šālôm* (wellbeing; Qumran Isaiah scroll reads 'good' here) and creating evil' (Isa. 45.6-7). Amos asks the rhetorical question: 'Does evil befall a city, unless Yahweh has done it?' (3.6). The prophetic books are filled with statements about the evil Yahweh does to people and places. In the writings of an élite devoted to a monist outlook where there is only one God, it is inevitable that the creation of evil should be attributed to Yahweh, who is the creator of everything.

Generally, evil in the biblical writings refers to disaster and misfortune, as well as to human wickedness. Hence Isaiah 45.7 balances 'wellbeing' or 'good fortune' (*šālôm*) with 'evil' or 'disaster' (*rāʿ*) to parallel the other opposites of 'darkness' and 'light'. Yahweh creates the polarities – in opposition perhaps to the Zoroastrian view that such opposites indicate a fundamental dualism in the nature of things. Although the view expressed in Isaiah 45.7 is considerably different from that stated in Genesis 1 (Elohim creates light and goodness and no mention is made of his having created darkness and misfortune), there is no other source for evil in the Hebrew Bible than God. All the disasters and terrible experiences which befall humans come from the one divine origin.

The polytheistic background to the Bible is peopled with gods, so disaster can be attributed to different deities, especially when the gods are so often represented as being in conflict with one another. Advanced religious cultures tend to have one high god who controls all the other gods, and usually this god is made responsible for disasters happening to the community (e.g. Zeus in Homer). Occasionally the Hebrew Bible retains a glimpse of this polytheistic world and blames the gods for wickedness perpetrated among humans (e.g. Psalm 82). A few stories indicate a shift away from making Yahweh responsible for communal disaster. These fix on a lesser figure within the divine council who is then delegated to savage and destroy individuals and communities. The Satan figure in Job 1—2 illustrates the motif in a paradigmatic fashion. As a member of the divine council chamber and as a lesser divinity himself, the Satan has the role of opposing or challenging people on behalf of Yahweh, but always as Yahweh's loyal and faithful servant. He is his master's voice. The terrible things he does to Job and to his family are by divine command and do not represent an independent will. In his speeches Job has no doubt that the source of his trouble, the one who gives the earth into the hands of the wicked, is Eloah (Job 9.13–24). But in the Hebrew Bible the figure of the Satan is too minor to be significant. A few fragments depict him in oppositional contexts: he and Yahweh's angel contend over Joshua the high priest (Zech. 3.1-2), and he is once credited with inciting David to do wrong (1 Chr. 21.1). This story of how David numbered Israel, thereby incurring divine anger against the nation – an anger which destroyed seventy thousand men of Israel – is interesting because it is part of a double account (or a reinterpretation?) of the same story with one important feature changed. In the version which appears in 2 Samuel 24 it is Yahweh who incites David to instigate a census of the people, because he is angry with Israel. The account in 1 Chronicles 21 has Satan stand against Israel and incite David to number the nation. A comparison of the two stories will introduce the reader to the intertextual niceties of reading the Bible.

An equation between Yahweh and Satan (in 1 Chronicles 21 the name is a proper name rather than a role as in Job and Zechariah) is one possible reading of the two stories. That is, Satan is one of the forms taken by Yahweh or is Yahweh's *alter ego*. A different approach would read the Chronicles text as a *re*interpretation of the story in Samuel in the light of a somewhat different account of causality embraced by the Chronicler. This viewpoint would see the Samuel account as being prior to that of Chronicles. While that is probably the majority opinion among biblical scholars on the relative order of the two scrolls, it is not necessarily entailed by the two stories. The difference might be due to the discrete locations of the production of the accounts. In the Chronicler's world the adversarial role of the opposer has developed in the direction of a somewhat malign personality, whereas for the writer of 2 Samuel 24, Yahweh's will is the only operative force in the world and so no mention is made of an underling. How these two different views relate to one another we cannot determine, because we know nothing about the writers nor about when or where they wrote. Whether the writer of the Samuel piece could have put a name on any of the members of the divine council, or even believed in such an entity, is also something we know nothing about. But the alternation of Yahweh with Satan or Satan with Yahweh is itself an interesting feature of these texts.

In the book of Jubilees – a work written in the second century BCE and associated now with the Pseudepigrapha – there is a splendid rewriting of Genesis and Exodus 1—12, with the biblical narrative enlarged and elaborated by means of extracts from the Sinaitic revelation to Moses. At two notable points in the narrative the writer clarifies the biblical text by introducing into the dramatic action the prince Mastema. In the first instance, it is as background to the story of the divine testing of Abraham (Gen. 22) where God's command to sacrifice Isaac is shown to be the outcome of a discussion between God and Mastema. Mastema suggests testing Abraham by means of commanding him to offer Isaac as a burnt-offering on the altar. Abraham's obedience to this divine command puts Mastema to shame. Thus the problem of how God could command Abraham to murder his son is modified by the introduction of a story rather similar to that in Job 1—2 (Jubilees 17.16—18.12). In the second instance, Mastema is made the person responsible for seeking to slay Moses in that strangest of incidents related in Exodus 4.24-26. Mastema is represented as the opponent of Moses and the one assisting the Egyptians during the fateful period before the exodus (Jubilees 48). Thus Satan and Mastema look like narratological or mythological devices for resolving what some writers saw as problems in the representation of God as being implicated in particularly heinous offences against people (Isaac, Job, Moses and the seventy thousand Israelites slaughtered because God incited David to hold a census). But it must be emphasized that most biblical writers had no difficulty in presenting Yahweh/Elohim as the author and source of evil.

The Satan figure is developed further in the apocalypses, in the New Testament and in the writings of various theologians in the early churches (especially Origen and Augustine). In the Gospels and the book of Revelation Satan appears as one of the (many) names of the Devil, a figure derived from extra-biblical mythology. If in the Hebrew Bible the Satan has a relatively innocent investigative role, with perhaps a more vicious strain in Chronicles, he may be said to border on the negative and destructive aspects of Yahweh's personality – a kind of J. Edgar Hoover (to use Neil Forsyth's analogue), with a tendency to think for himself which makes him easily assimilated in Christian thought with other forms of the mythology of evil. As there is remarkably little said in the Hebrew Bible about this Satan figure, his origins, lineaments and activities have to be derived from ancient Near Eastern mythology and classical myths. The monsters and dragons of Sumerian, Akkadian and Babylonian myths provide the necessary background and the writings of the book of Enoch, Irenaeus, Origen and Augustine supply the sufficient conditions for the creation of the Devil (the great Gothic deity of medieval Christendom). To this creation the Bible offers very little except for a few names. But in the period between Origen and the Reformation the Bible was to be read by Christian theologians in the light of the Devil as a regulative principle.

Evil in Christian theology

Among the many serious differences between the Hebrew Bible and the New Testament – differences which make their conjoining in the Christian Bible a most curious hermeneutic phenomenon – the role of the Devil and the demonic in the New Testament will strike the well-read reader as one of the most obvious. While there are demons, magical forces and mysterious entities on the margins of the Hebrew

Bible, they are kept well under control by the ideological constraints of the writers. It is otherwise with the New Testament. The demonic is a more virulent force than the Spirit (the upper-case 'S' may be contentious here) in the sense that the power represented by demons is more statistically significant for its writers. The notion expressed in Ephesians 6.12 – 'For we are not contending against flesh and blood, but against the principalities, against the powers, against the world rulers of this present darkness, against the spiritual hosts of wickedness in the heavenly places' – typifies the background and subtext of the New Testament. In Luke's account of the betrayal of Jesus the story is introduced by the statement 'Then Satan entered into Judas called Iscariot' (22.3), thus turning the death of Jesus into a cosmic conspiracy. Thus the earliest of Christian writings breathe an atmosphere of the diabolical and the demonic which may well account for the emphasis placed on the Devil and all his works in the formative centuries of Christian thought.

In the construction of orthodox Christian theology (in the fourth to sixth centuries) the Devil plays a large role, and over the first thousand years of the churches the doctrine of the atonement has the Devil as a prime element (the Christus Victor myth). Beliefs about the Devil, the fall of mankind (a specifically Christian reading of Genesis 2—3), and original sin (an Augustinian reading of Genesis 3) provided Christian thought with an answer to the old classical question, 'whence evil?'. Ancient rebellion against God, either human or superhuman, brought evil into the universe and exonerated God from being the author of that evil. So the churches had no need to attribute the origins of evil to God, because they possessed a hermeneutic of evil which owed nothing to the assertion of Isaiah 45.7 that Yahweh had created evil. Of course, what the Hebrew Bible meant by evil was nothing like the radical evil at the heart of things typical of the apocalypses and New Testament demonism. For the writers of the Hebrew scriptures, evil was profoundly concrete. It referred to disaster and misfortune in the community, or to the evil deeds of the wicked. Perhaps in Genesis 6.5 evil takes on an abstract quality, but even there it remains something which occurs in the human mind (this is not yet Kant's notion of radical evil, though it might be viewed as beginning to move in the direction of Kantian evil). But in Jewish thought human evil arises from the fact that God created in human beings the impulse to do evil as well as the impulse to do good. The possibility of evil arises out of the world God has made, and therefore in some very real sense God is the author of evil. In later kabbalistic thought evil may be more inadvertent than that, but it remains connected to God. Christian thinking about evil owes more to Greek philosophy and mythology than it does to the Bible, in spite of the uses made of Genesis 2—3 in the development of Christian theology.

The application of a Christian hermeneutic

The differences between the two parts of the Christian Bible on the subject of evil and the fundamental cleavage between Jewish and Christian thinking on the question 'whence evil?' provide good examples of why the Bible is so problematic for Christian theology. As the New Testament writings come out of a different background from those of the Hebrew Bible, it is hardly to be wondered at that the two collections of books should have different opinions on some subjects. They belong to distinctive linguistic worlds, employ very different hermeneutics and concern themselves with un-common matters. The logic and rhetoric of the Hebrew Bible lead on through Qumran and the Mishna to the Talmuds, Midrashim and rabbinic commentaries. Emergent churches develop gospels and letters, commentaries and treatises which, combined with Greek philosophy, give rise to the hermeneutic masterpieces of classic Christian theology. In order to incorporate the Septuagint into the construction of Christian theology, fundamental transformations of the text were required. Philo, a first-century (CE) Jew, showed by means of Greek allegorical method how the scriptures could be given a meaning other than the plain meaning of the text. But the Christian transformation of the Hebrew Bible went far beyond the allegorical reinterpretation of ancient texts. It transposed the text into so many different new keys that the original meaning of the text was lost until the rise of critical theology in the seventeenth century.

Reading against the plain meaning of a text creates problems for modern historically-minded people. Imposing on the text a completely foreign hermeneutic can also be regarded as an illegitimate approach to reading. Since the development of the critical study of the Bible, the competent reader is inevitably uneasy with anachronistic reading strategies which subvert history in favour of some propagandist reading of texts. Under certain conditions such readings may be tolerated or pursued for a variety of purposes, but it is generally recognized today that treating the Hebrew Bible as if it had been written by Christians is both wrong and unhistorical. Yet until the rise of critical theology such a concern with the historical was much less important than other matters. The literal and historical meanings of texts were granted a certain place in the interpretation of the Bible, but allegorical and christological readings were more important. The great diversity of writings within the Bible means that no consistent representation of any particular subject is to be found. This lack of consistency, with its concomitant lack of coherence, undermines the philosophical-theological quest for simplicity and clarity of meaning. A God who creates evil will not sit easily with a theological account of evil designed to exonerate God from responsibility for evil. Thus, if what the Hebrew Bible has to say is taken seriously, Hebrew statement and Christian theology will make poor bedfellows.

A critical reading of the Bible may be able to resolve some of the problems of diversity in the text by recognizing the different provenances of parts of the book and the inevitability of contrary opinions in literature produced over a lengthy period of time. The figurative nature of much of the language in the Bible makes it highly unsuitable for theologizing. Here Greek philosophy gave Christian writers the impetus to turn some of that language into theological concepts, but at the expense of biblical metaphor. A book which can depict God as never sleeping (Ps. 121.4), as an early riser (a Hebrew idiom lost in the translation: Jer. 7.25; 25.3), and as one who must wake up (Ps. 44.23; Isa. 51.9) is congenitally unsuited as a source for doing theology. The very nature of biblical language militates against a philosophical-theological reading of the Bible. This seems to be the real deformation of biblical language by the early Christian theologians: they took the biblical metaphors literally and turned them into substantive notions. Much of Augustine's treatment of scripture suffers from this technique.

Of course it is understandable that Christian writers using the scriptures should transform (or deform) them in various ways, because taken by themselves they would not have yielded suitable meanings for christological purposes. Origen, who in many ways saved the scriptures for the churches, recognized that the divine wisdom had concealed hidden mysteries under the covering of history and narratives in the scriptures, yet had also introduced impossibilities and incongruities into the text in order to make the reader recognize the need to follow a more sublime road so as to discover the divine wisdom (*De Principiis*, Book IV, ch. I, §§ 14-15). But once the text is turned into a code which can only be deciphered by having access to a privileged key, the book is taken from the realm of rational discourse and assigned to the magical circle of the initiated. This is undoubtedly one use to which the Bible may be put, but in the hands of the classically trained exegetes and rhetoricians such as Origen and Augustine the obscurities of scripture became an aesthetics of obscurity rather than, as in Jewish exegesis, the possibility of multiple meanings.

To return to the metaphors of the sleeping habits of God mentioned as an example of the figurativeness of biblical language, it should be said that so many different metaphors used of God provide for a diversity of theological interpretations. Such a diversity makes the formulation of one fundamental theology of the Bible impossible. Semitic habits of expression delight in multiple metaphors darting in every direction, and hyperbolic descriptions which literal-minded readers read at their peril. At the same time the representation of the deity as an actor in the human scene entails a causality of explanation which must offend the theological mind. Thus Ezekiel represents Yahweh as saying that he made the Israelites sacrifice their children by fire and gave them statutes that were not good (20.25-26). Jeremiah, on the other hand, denies that the burning of the children was by divine command (7.31). Simple contradictions no doubt, but no theologian could take Ezekiel seriously and insist on the goodness of God at the same time. To the reader trained in the critical method and lacking a dogma of biblical inspiration, the statements of Ezekiel and Jeremiah can be taken as different representations of the divine *by the human*. As such they represent something of the diversity of scripture, a diversity as natural as it is human. Both the diversity and the figurative language, however, should warn the intelligent reader of the problems of reading scripture for the purposes of doing theology.

A God who sleeps and does not sleep, yet who rises early in the morning as if he were a traveller or trader who had to load up the pack animals before setting off on the day's business (the force of the Hebrew metaphor used in Jeremiah and elsewhere), is very much a human construct determined by figurative language. These are graphic ways of describing the activity or inactivity of a god (cf. Elijah's jeering tones in 1 Kgs 18.27). They are statements about the relationship between the deity and the community under the constraints of specific situations. The unsleeping god is a metaphor of continual divine protection, whereas the sleeping god metaphor expresses the community's sense of the absence of divine presence (i.e. protection). The early rising god figure of speech has its meaning qualified by whatever verb is associated with it (e.g. sending prophets, warning, etc.) and indicates either the deity's intense concern to communicate something to the community or his persistence over a long time (Jer. 25.3) in a particular course of action. None of the distinctive metaphors should be isolated from such communal relationships and turned into an abstract principle about the divine, as if any one such metaphor were somehow a literal statement about the nature of divinity. If Yahweh is made to represent the eternal, living God (a considerable jump in assumptions and requiring a book-length set of arguments as warrants) then these metaphors will lose their essential usefulness. For God neither sleeps nor wakes, loves nor hates, is angry or caring. These are human descriptions applied to the divine because divinity can only be spoken of by using metaphors and other figurative language. When philosophically-minded theologians get their hands on Bibles there is a terrible tendency for the metaphoric to be turned into the substantive and for the figurative to become abstracted into theology.

While the beginnings of this tendency can be detected in the Septuagint translation of the Hebrew Bible (e.g. the revelation of the divine name in Exodus 3.14 is easily ontologized in the Greek, so that ontology rears its ugly head in a text innocent of ontology), and is developed further in the New Testament representation of Jesus as the only begotten son of the father (John 1.14), it should be resisted because it imposes an alien transformation on the reading of the biblical text. It cannot be avoided in the theological development of the churches because Greek philosophy was one of the prime creators of Christian theology, but its imposition on the Bible conceals the considerable gap between that collection of writings and its reception in later times.

The hidden God

Among the many different metaphors which are used to describe the relationship between Yahweh and the community, the one I have singled out for this chapter (but have so far failed to use!) is that of the hiding God. The hiddenness of God occurs as a motif in a number of different places in the Bible, and raises some interesting points for discussion. In some ways it may be regarded as an alternative way of talking about the sleeping God, but it has an undercurrent of deliberation about it which gives it greater force than talk about a soporific deity. The *locus classicus* of the metaphor appears in Isaiah 45.15 where it is stated: 'Truly, you are a God who hides yourself, O God of Israel, the saviour.' This verse was the inspiration for Pascal's observation cited as an epigraph to this chapter, and he quotes its Vulgate form, *Vere tu es deus absconditus*. The Pascalian notion of the *deus absconditus*, 'the hidden god', has particular resonances of the seventeenth century which belong to the history of ideas and which need not concern us here; but his point about the falseness of religion which fails to acknowledge the divine hiddenness is worth keeping to the fore. As a statement in Isaiah 40—55 the saying has as its context the liturgical hymns of the second temple (Persian period or even later). It is unclear from its immediate context who the speaker might be, and therefore the precise weight to give the words is unknown. It could be something said by the wealthy merchants of foreign nations or it could be a response of Israel to the confession made by those merchants (45.14). The statement seems to be confessional, and combines the admission of hiddenness with the acknowledgement of the deity as saviour. In such a context the notion of hiddenness may refer to the devious way in which the deity works, either as one hidden from the other nations or as one whose way is concealed from his own people. It is a confession of mystification. But it is also a recognition (accusation?) of the self-concealment of God: it is not a statement about divine hiddenness as such but an assertion that God (deliberately) hides himself (the Hebrew verb formation is reflexive).

A book-length study could be written on this topic and the various Hebrew words which depict the hiding god, so a few pages in passing are not going to be able to explore the metaphor adequately. The notion of divine hiding appears most frequently, as one would expect, in the book of Psalms where worshippers and petitioners appeal to a silent, absent being whose hiddenness is the ground of their perplexity (cf. Ps. 10.1; 13.1; 27.9; 69.17; 88.14; 102.2; 104.29; 143.7). It is clearly the equivalent of the sleeping god metaphor and appears as such in one of the great lament psalms in the Bible (44.23–24). In some cases Yahweh is said to hide his face because the people have sinned against him (e.g. Deut. 31.17–18; 32.20; Mic. 3.4; Isa. 57.17; 59.2; Jer. 33.5; Ezek. 39.23–24). In other cases the metaphor describes situations where Yahweh is absent or thought to be absent (cf. Gen. 4.14; Ps. 10.11). There is also the appeal to Yahweh to hide his face from the petitioner's sins (Ps. 51.9), which is another way of appealing for forgiveness. The lament contained in Isaiah 63.7—64.12 includes, among many other images, the hiddenness motif (64.7). This lament is a subtle working of traditional themes interwoven with complaints about the state of the community. In it are statements which move beyond the formal acknowledgement of human rebelliousness (63.10) to the recognition that it is Yahweh who causes the people to err (63.17, contrast 3.12) and hardens the communal mind (63.17 cf. 6.10). Divine anger *precedes* human sin (64.5) and the hiding of the divine face gives the people over into the power of their sins (64.7, the Hebrew here is obscure).

The mixture of confession of guilt and perplexity at the divine absence is characteristic of many of the biblical laments and makes them subtly different from those liturgical outpourings which wallow in guilt and confession (e.g. Ezra 9; Dan. 9). In Isaiah 54.8 the speaker makes Yahweh admit that he had momentarily hidden his face from the people in an outburst of anger (a moment which might be said to have lasted seventy years or many centuries, depending on perspective and when Isaiah should be dated); and the metaphor of hiding is used to describe the atrocities of the Babylonian destruction of Jerusalem, the deportations to Babylonia and all the concomitant severities of life lived under the conditions of a blighted economy. The other significant usage of the hiddenness motif in Isaiah occurs in 8.17, where the speaker admits to waiting for Yahweh who is described as 'hiding his face from the house of Jacob'; the reference in the next verse to Yahweh of hosts 'who dwells on Mount Zion' may put that hiddenness into perspective or may belong to the complexities of the redaction of the book of Isaiah, especially in relation to chapters 6 to 8.

The highly imagistic use of the metaphor of divine hiding combines all the anthropomorphic language of the Bible. It represents a god who has face and eyes and whose social mores reflect the emperor or king's gestures of averting or turning the face to the petitioner. The god's face needs to be mollified in appeasement (an image at home in the ritual of sacrifice) or sought in petition. When all is going well for the community or the individual, Yahweh may be said to have made his face shine on them and to have lifted up his face on them (Numbers 6.25–26). Such images describe the divine blessing and protection of the people. When disaster (evil) befalls the community, then Yahweh may be said to have withdrawn his presence or to have hidden his face from it. Whether the wickedness of the people or of individuals among them or other unknown causes are responsible for that divine absence is a matter for further determination. Hence the hiding of the face or of the divine self is another way of talking about the age-old question, 'whence evil?' And that question invariably has Yahweh somewhere in its answer.

Such anthropomorphic language is an inevitable part of the need to use metaphor when talking about the divine. It does however sit uneasily with philosophical conceptualizing, which is the heart of theological method. Different clusters of metaphors focus the attention on the divine in various ways which theologizing finds difficult to articulate without rejecting some and developing others. This makes the Bible a very untidy book for theologians. Its embarrassment of riches defies the pigeonholing so beloved of the philosophical-theological category-maker. A god who loves and hates, makes and destroys, sleeps and does not sleep, even rises early, changes his mind regularly, rages against and blesses, and is generally unpredictable in behaviour, is a mythic formation which does not lend itself easily to the formulations of classical theology. That entails a serious gap between the language of the Bible and the things theologians try to do with the Bible. What makes that gap part of the problem focused on in this book is the need of theological enterprise to discard much of the biblical language in order to carve out of it a coherent, consistent account. This is not necessarily a problem for theology itself, but it is highly problematic for any theology which reckons with using the Bible. The sheer unsuitability of the Bible as a source from which to do (philosophical) theology has been known for a long time – Spinoza has splendidly analyzed it – but Christian theology has inherited the Bible from a different culture and has nailed itself to that cross. Theology may function happily without the Bible because it does not need the Bible in order to do its work, but where it is yoked (unequally) with the Bible, then it will struggle in vain to accommodate all the Bible's anarchic language.

A quick reading of many books which combine Bible and theology may give the impression that the matter is by no means problematic.

Presumably the writers of such books are of the firm conviction that theology and Bible are ideal bedfellows. My own sense of the problematic, as I have indicated, relates to the totality of biblical language, the cultural worlds from which it came, and the alterity (otherness) of the books constituting the Bible – whichever testament or version is under discussion. (I would not deny that parts of the Bible can be harnessed to produce a kind of conformity to certain theological systems of thought, but it is what is excluded from such amalgams which concerns me here.) Systems of thought derived from philosophical interests and influences foreign to the Bible are not perhaps the best means of understanding or appreciating it. At the same time, by emphasizing the contradictory and contrary nature of many things in the Bible I want to underline the fact that contrarieties do not facilitate the production of coherent, consistent theologies. A God who hides himself may not be the most obvious image for a theology of revelation to use!

Images relating to the hiddenness of God – hence the hidden problematic of this chapter's title – constitute only a small part of the Hebrew Bible. They cannot be said to be an alternative to more dominant images of a deity who reveals himself in story and narrative, event, and encounter in many books of the Bible. What does, however, approach the oxymoronic is the claim that it is part of the divine revelation that Yahweh is hidden. One could understand the formulation 'it is the hidden god who reveals himself' to mean that the deity believed to be hidden has now revealed himself. That would make sense. But a revelation which revealed the hiddenness of the deity would be at best a paradox (where oxymoron is not allowable in theological discourse) and more likely a contradiction of any normal sense of the word 'revelation'. Of course the Bible does not assert such a thing, and the hiddenness motif is not part of the narratives which tell of encounters with the divine self-revelation.

How these two should be related to each other (if they should be grouped together in the same discourse in the first place) is a difficult question. The big story in the Hebrew Bible has to do with Yahweh's self-revelation at the burning bush and then at Sinai. Apart from the smokescreen at Sinai, hiddenness is not the best description of either event. On the other hand, though the category 'revelation' is one used by readers to describe the stories, a close reading of the biblical text will reveal that the writers are reluctant to represent the deity as being visible. Exodus 24.9–11 asserts that a few named individuals and seventy representatives of the people *saw God*; but generally Yahweh cannot be seen. His face is not for seeing, though parts of him may be visible (cf. Exod. 33.18–23). What seems to constitute the 'revelation' of Sinai is the proclamation of the terms of the covenant and the organization of the cultus. It is a hearing rather than a seeing. No form is seen, only a voice is heard (Deut. 4.12) and that voice soon moves on to speak only to Moses rather than to the people (Exod. 20.19; Deut. 5.5; though the 'face to face' of Deut. 5.4 is problematic).

The model of this divine revelation would appear to be that of prophetic discourse. Yahweh speaks to the prophet who in turn speaks to the people: Yahweh speaks to Moses who speaks to the people. Visions, even of Yahweh (cf. Isa. 6), are part of the divine disclosures to prophets, and there are elements of the vision in the Sinai story. The reverse of this kind of divine communication would be divine silence or absence. But in the way the biblical story has been constructed around the formation of the cultus at Sinai and the declaration of covenant stipulations (e.g. Exod. 21—23), there really can be no divine silence or absence. Once given, the divine *tōrâh* (a Hebrew word which does badly in translation: try something paraphrastic like 'the terms and conditions under which life with God may be lived') cannot, by definition, be rescinded.

The metaphor of hiddenness relates not to divine instructions but to that appalling sense of absence in the community caused by the devastations of invading forces, plague, disaster and all the other misfortunes human beings are prey to. In Deuteronomy Yahweh hides from the community because of breaches of the covenant (31.17–18). In the lament psalms the hiddenness is not caused by offences against the covenant (Ps. 44.17–24), though it is recognized that Yahweh may have renounced the covenant (Ps. 89.39). It is that detachment of the hiddenness motif from breaches of the covenant which gives the metaphor its resonance in the biblical laments. This is no quid pro quo or double entry in a cosmic book-keeping enterprise. It is one expression among many of a deep existential horror in a situation beyond human control or explanation. As such it sits uneasily with language of revelation or in religions which make much of primal revelatory events – though it tallies perfectly with human experience whatever the religious discourse (or lack of it) used.

Pascal's use of the Isaiah 45.15 text incorporates it into the

teaching of the Christian religion; though Pascalian theology is an
acquired taste not to everybody's liking (Jansenism had something to
do with his theology and that also was a rather unpleasant
development of Augustinian thought). Pascal was not a brilliant reader
of the Old Testament because he was too eager to use it for apologetic
purposes; and his reading of prophecy was, while quite traditional,
frankly awful from a critical or rational perspective. His reflections
on rabbinic thought do him no credit either. As his *Pensées* are by
their nature fragmentary, with only a few developed at any length, it
is not easy to articulate his notion of the hidden God beyond the few
words he has written on the subject. His use of the biblical *proposition*
(for such it is when considered out of its context in Isaiah 45) relates
to God's wish to hide himself and thereby make the true religion less
than manifest. As the Christian religion teaches that God hides
himself, it shows itself to be true. Pascal has no real sense of the
biblical metaphor of the hiddenness of God, nor of the way it is used
to express a deep sense of surprise in Isaiah 45 or of anguish
(*Anfechtung/Angst* of a Kierkegaardian nature) in the laments. But I
have used Pascal's famous citation of Isaiah 45.15 as an epigraphic
introduction to this chapter in order to draw attention to what has
been regarded as an important feature of religion and how it also
constitutes part of the problematic of the Bible for theology.

Karl Barth's treatment of the hiddenness theme is a much more
developed affair than Pascal's. Barth recognizes the principle of
God's hiddenness as a statement of faith (i.e. as equivalent to a
confessional stance as appears to be the case in Isa. 45.15). It is in
faith itself, as he says, that we are forced to acknowledge that
knowledge of God *begins* with the knowledge of his hiddenness. In a
sense he treats the hiddenness theme as a revelation in itself rather
than as the community's response to its own experiences or as a
reflection on specific events or experiences as the biblical writers use
the metaphor. This is quite distinct from the biblical usage of the
term and should be viewed as an individual, gifted theologian's
adaptation for his own purposes of a biblical image. It chimes in with
his opposition to natural theology (his *bête noire*) in that it allows him
to start from God's hiddenness rather than from the biblical sense of
God's manifestation in the world (e.g. Ps. 19.1-4; Isa. 6.3). Also, it
fits into his fideistic scheme of things because it is treated, not as a
reflection of what is obvious from observing the world at large, but as
a given of revealed religion. Both Pascal and Barth use the

hiddenness theme in accordance with their own particular theological systems of thought, without seriously engaging with the biblical metaphor or its range. (That is not a serious criticism of the theologians, because they are entitled to use biblical tags for whatever purposes they wish. But it does help to illustrate the claim running through this book of how awkwardly the Bible fits into general theological discussion.)

The different parts of the Bible are not easily combined together because the diversity of images encourages breadth of development rather than consistency or coherence. The hidden god, like the sleeping god, is not a principle of revelation (unlike Pascal or Barth's use of the idea) but a way of describing communal experiences. If it is turned into a regulative principle it will undermine talk about revelation (whatever the content of that word may be). It may of course be used to deconstruct all biblical discourse about revelation, or the correspondence between obedience to the covenant and divine protection – in the lament psalms that possibility is mooted but neither developed nor highlighted. God's elusiveness has been identified as a central element in the Bible, and this would make connections with the hiddenness motif. But the general presentation of the Bible – this applies to both testaments – tends towards a confident assertion of God's existence and his presence in the community. His hiddenness is on the margins of the traditions (the literature associated with Wisdom may have a different reading of this possibility, especially the books of Job and Qoheleth), just where social reality is beginning to break into the rhetoric of religion. The New Testament writers' conviction that in Jesus the invisible God has been made manifest runs counter to the hiddenness theme. Such confidence as is expressed by the prologue to the Fourth Gospel – e.g. 'we have beheld his glory' (1.14) – hardly admits of a dimension of the hidden, let alone of the hiddenness of God. There is such a celebration of divine presence in the New Testament that the theme of hiddenness appears only to bear on human behaviour (e.g. Matt. 6.1–6). Triumphalism is such among the writers that Paul can explain the failure of his gospel among certain people to be due to the (conspiratorial) fact that the god of this world has blinded the minds of the unbelievers in order to keep them 'from seeing the light of the gospel of the glory of Christ, who is the likeness of God' (2 Cor. 4.3–4). Everything in that statement speaks against hiddenness.

So the problematic God whose hiddenness is equally problematic is not a New Testament theme. That may only indicate a lack of time and experience among the early churches which had yet to find any need for such a metaphor. On the other hand, much of the gospel representation of Jesus of Nazareth suggests a hiddenness – a figure incognito as it were – which makes the modern reader question all that rhetoric of manifestation (see Chapter Four). Of course, the metaphor of the hidden God need not be used throughout the Bible. It is a metaphor which expresses a number of responses to perplexing situations, and such predicaments are not usually the dominant concerns of the élites who put the biblical books together. As an important subtext of parts of the Bible I have used it as a means for reflecting on some aspects of the problematic nature of the Bible for theology. To develop it further would be to overstate the case or deconstruct theology completely.

3
The Chimera of
Biblical Christianity

The Christian's Bible is a drug store. Its contents remain the same; but the medical practice changes.

Mark Twain

From a juxtaposition of this kind nothing but shocks and collisions can come.

Matthew Arnold

Is the Bible enough for us? In these days, I believe, Jesus himself would say to those who sit down in a state of *melancholy*, It is not here, get up and go forth. Why do you seek the living among the dead?

Vincent van Gogh

Pascal's famous opposition of the God of Abraham, Isaac and Jacob to the God of the philosophers states the problem of the Bible for theology at its strongest level. Most Christian communities and churches have preferred either a weaker case of that opposition or a position which denied the essential truth of Pascal's mystical encounter in favour of the Dodo's incorporative principle by which everybody wins – granting equal status to Bible, theology, reason, tradition, and so on. The Bible's role in modern theology would best be described as an auxiliary source for theology (*ancilla theologiae*), especially as a supplier of images, metaphors and a pool of insightful phrases. But however its role is defined (in whichever version may be preferred), and whatever hierarchical status is granted it within a complex network of important constituent factors contributing to a multiplicity of different Jewish and Christian identities, it will always be only part of the intellectual holdings of any religious community. This is how it has always worked since its construction *as the Bible* in the fourth to sixth centuries (somewhat earlier for Jewish communities). After all, as we have noted, the Christian churches existed for centuries before the New Testament was created – and significant changes have occurred since then in terms of situations, hermeneutics, development and the modernization of Western civilization. The texts may remain, everything else changes; and therefore the texts are changed. They are changed as to meaning and significance, and as to their relative situation within any particular nexus of beliefs and practices. How we read (ancient) texts changes all the time, and is determined by time and culture as much as by situational and existential changes in our own lives. Thus a map of the history of the reception of the Bible, especially of the period since the sixteenth century, would be very complicated to produce and would vary for each individual reader and receiving community. Such large-scale charts, indicative of the range and depth of biblical interpretation over the centuries, constitute good warrants for pluralist readings of the Bible today. They also militate against any prescriptivist account of how the Bible should be read. Of the making of readings of the Bible there is no end. Nor should there be. Books with single meanings – if such things exist – have no future.

Reading and interpretation

These brief observations of a general nature must serve as the introduction to a chapter on reading the Bible within Christian cultures. As there are so many different ways of reading any version of the Bible (at least as many readings as there are readers) it is not possible to provide an account of all, or even many, of the different ways of reading it. At home in the critical reading of the Bible, I want to make some observations on the problem of reading with reference to a different mode of discourse applied to the Bible.

The problem of reading is something every reader of a book confronts: what do texts mean? what is being said here and why? how do I read this text *now*? how do I relate to it? The questions are manifold but they are all part of the complex process of hermeneutics. When different readings of the 'same' text ('same' as a qualifier here can be a weasel word because the readers of the text do not always share the same background, perspective, values or experience) are analyzed, the importance of the hermeneutic frameworks used and the social or cultural contexts in which the readings are done become obvious. Whether the Bible is read using as the interpretative framework the creeds of conciliar Christianity, or the confessions of the Reformed churches, or the Book of Mormon, or Mary Baker Eddy's *Science and Health* (1875), the meaning given to it will always be a specific reading of it and all the readings will be different. One cannot therefore rule out all readings but one's own without being guilty of lopsided reading and chauvinism. There are, so far as I can see, no privileged frameworks of reading, though there may well be more appropriate or better readings dependent on the arguments used to support them.

Reading texts is both a simple and a complex process of human activity. Telephone directories are relatively easy to read and philosophical books are relatively difficult. The relativities will vary from person to person: some people will find the writings of Albert Einstein or Martin Heidegger easy and a joy to read, others will be completely mystified by either writer. Some readers will find comics or Agatha Christie a delight, others will find either or both unreadable. These relativities could be multiplied beyond necessity, but they make the point which applies to the Bible as much as to any collection of books. In some ways the Bible shares with all ancient writings the further difficulties of alien thought in alien languages from alien times. The alterity of the Bible cannot be minimized, though in a very real sense all books are other than their readers. Where the otherness of the Bible is important, however, is in Christian cultures where it has been domesticated for centuries (see Chapter Five). Outside philosophy neither Plato nor Aristotle has been domesticated, so their works are still capable of illuminating us after serious study. The Bible suffers from a surfeit of readers reading in an adulatory fashion, and so its otherness has become alienated from it in Western consciousness. Further difficulties in interpreting alien languages, with their concomitant alien thought forms, also apply to the Bible. Its domestication robs it of much of its alien qualities and so impoverishes our readings of it. All these factors have been emphasized already in Chapter One, but reminding the reader of them will do no harm. They contribute to making the reading of the Bible today both complex and problematic.

Reading, teaching, studying, translating, writing and reflecting on the Bible in academic, intellectual and cultural contexts gives me access to it in its different versions at many levels. Familiarity with the long histories of Jewish, Christian, humanist and rationalist interpretations of the book in all its manifestations provides me with a wide knowledge of the range of possible readings generated by individuals and communities over many centuries. As the intellectual property of so many different and discrete communities, the Bible is clearly a generator of multiple readings. Yet it also retains the integrity of collections of texts *not* produced by the communities using it. There is a sense in which the biblical text is over against, or outside the community, and may be said to act as a constraint on the readings derived from or imposed on it. Such a constraining factor is typical of all books, though the weight given to the text as outsider (i.e. as an objective entity within the community and over against the subjectivity of reader or group) in any particular reading, is a matter difficult to determine. As a critical reader of texts, including the Bible, I find it hard to quantify the contributions of subjectivity-objectivity to any one reading of a specific text. Reading is such a subtle blend of both aspects, text and thinker, that it is easier to recognize a good reading when one encounters it than to define it theoretically. Hence I can appreciate a multiplicity of different readings of the Bible while occasionally (or often as the case may be) having to turn away from some readings because they appear to me to be such awful abuses of the text, as well as travesties of the reading process. 'This is not how texts should be read,' is my reaction to *bad* readings.

Now it would take a much longer and a rather different book to spell out all the moves in determining good from bad readings and justifying the part intuitive, part rational judgement involved in making such assessments. I will, however, endeavour in this chapter to illustrate by argument some of the ways of reading the Bible which I would count as constituting a bad (i.e. poor) reading of the text.

Christianity is an abstraction which may be defined in many different ways, depending on the perspective of the person doing the defining. The beliefs and practices which make up Christendom (an older, more general term for Christianity) were developed over many centuries and, in many senses, may be said to be developing still. Christianity as a way of life and a system of thought is still evolving. Various historical forms of it may wish to think of themselves as representative of 'true' Christianity, but the diversity of Christian belief and practice over almost two thousand years now defies such chauvinism. At one end of the spectrum may be forms of vatican I style Roman Catholicism and at the other end may be Quaker, Inner Light and Mennonite forms; or the spectrum can be arranged in a different way, having snake-handling fundamentalists at one end and forms of Christian Buddhism (typified by the amiable Anglican Don Cupitt) at the other. The multitudinous protesting and Protestant sects which were generated by the Reformation must also be included in any reliable spectrum, though exactly where they should be situated on it is a matter for much debate. Also, the many new movements which have developed since the beginning of the nineteenth century (e.g. Mormons, Jehovah's Witnesses, Christadelphians, etc.) belong to the Christian spectrum of religion.

All too often there is a tendency to identify one branch of the Christian churches with Christianity to the exclusion of all others. A notion of 'orthodoxy' still survives the many fundamental changes in Western culture, as if the definitions of one group should be regarded as normative for other groups. This may be how Constantinian religion developed in its persecution of groups subsequently judged not to be orthodox, but it is not how the Christian churches first developed, or continue to develop in many different times and places. Defining one's own group as the only true version of Christianity is the mark of the sect, even when it assigns to itself all the hallmarks of orthodoxy. In the long history of Western (Roman Catholic) and Eastern (Orthodox) and Reformed (Calvinist, Lutheran, etc.) forms of Christianity, diversity of belief and practice would appear to be the only unifying quality discernible. (I overstate the case a little here. Of course what makes a group, movement, church or whatever, Christian rather than something else, must be some form of relation to Jesus. The following of Jesus and the worship of God in relation to the teachings of Jesus are inevitably bound up with the definition of Christianity.)

Even the attempt to define what Christianity is – never mind what it was – poses many problems, and no brief account of the matter will appeal to Christians in general. That having been acknowledged, I must still persevere in regarding as Christian every group which claims or has claimed such an epithet for itself. To do otherwise would be to become sectarian, as well as being selective and imposing my definition on others. I am too aware of the many different forms of Christian belief and practice, as well as of the diversity of communities, throughout Christian history to imagine for one moment that there ever was or will be one solitary, single defining process which would or could specify who is or is not Christian. Even a cursory reading of the New Testament will demonstrate the great diversity of viewpoints and groups in the earliest centuries of the emergent churches. As the centuries unfolded the groups multiplied and the diversity increased. A glance around the world today will reveal an ever-increasing diversification of Christian communities, beliefs and practices.

The shibboleth of 'biblical Christianity'

Having set my remarks in context I must now identify a modern form of reading the Bible which strikes me as being a poor reading of the text. As such it illustrates much of what I have been trying to put across about the problem of the Bible for theology. In my general reading of popular journalism dealing with religious matters and in listening to the mass media (radio especially, but religion on television also contributes), I keep encountering the peculiar phrase 'biblical Christianity'. It is quite a recent coinage and its meaning is not always made clear by the speakers using it. Judging by what is said by people for whom the term appears to have significance, it seems to mean something like 'the Christianity believed in and practised by the writers of the Bible'. Or it may mean, 'Those bits of Christian belief and practice which are in conformity to the Bible should be encouraged and all other forms avoided.' Whatever its precise meaning – it is used by different groups of people so may not have any specific meaning as such – it seems to function as a shibboleth which identifies 'us' and 'them'. Like all shibboleths it is used by those who identify the phrase as representing everything they stand for and as a shorthand way of denigrating those who hold different viewpoints. Its vagueness, no doubt, is also part of its charm. It combines two hurrah words – Bible, Christianity – and functions as a slogan for action. Like all activists' slogans it is probably stronger on emotive connotation than on denotation. It is a rallying-to standard designed to whip up commitment. As such it appears to be as political a phrase as it is ideological.

I have picked out this particular phrase because I am genuinely puzzled by its semantic force, as much as by its political incoherence.

To hear different individuals talking about something called 'biblical Christianity', and usually in a context of social action, is to be set to wondering about the social phenomenon behind such talk. In many cases the phrase is used in an authoritarian way by people who appear to want to force whatever they understand by it on other people. It is political talk. It is also social engineering. It is political lobbying by religious factions within a modern democracy. In a pluralist democracy all groups are fully entitled to function as pressure groups in order to contribute to public debate in the determining of how we should live in society. But since pluralistic societies cannot be shaped by one faction to the exclusion of all other groups, such pressure groups may well constitute serious problems for the wellbeing of democratic society. If, in addition, the philosophy behind their belief system is incoherent, then the political life of the community may be damaged by such movements. So the matter may not only be an issue in reading texts but also one of some consequence for the organization of communal life. As is so very often the case, the textual is the political.

What makes the phrase 'biblical Christianity' incoherent is its meaninglessness. It has no historical meaning, whatever it may signify to people who use it. As a series of historical movements Christianity (an abstraction) came into being over many, many centuries. It is not possible to say how many centuries, because different forms of Christianity are still evolving. If we arbitrarily limit the centuries to a specific number, who is to say how many? When should we stop and say, 'Ah, now Christianity is completely formed'? After the fourth century, or the sixth century, or how about the tenth century? The great conciliar decisions which shaped orthodox Christianity – one quite dominant form – were only the beginning of the formalization of doctrinal issues, and the schism between East and West soon gave them rather different developmental frameworks.

But even if we were to make the councils the determinative criteria of orthodoxy, that would hardly help the Bible. All the various collections of books constituting the Bibles of different communities were written considerably before the formulations of the councils and creeds. The conciliar decisions helped to create a specific hermeneutic for reading the New Testament which gave it its place in the orthodox scheme of things. Some elements in parts of the New Testament writings may have contributed to the development of that orthodox framework, but many elements did not. On the basis of conciliar orthodoxy many of the New Testament writings (or writers) might well have been judged unorthodox; but the arrow of time flies in only one direction. When, in the late fourth century, the canonical list of New Testament writings began to take on a fixed form, and many writings which had enjoyed relative importance for various communities were discriminated against, we have a particular kind of ideological control of scriptures. The factors involved in this very complex growth of the Christian canon were manifold and include economic and political as much as religious considerations. It took centuries for a particular canon to be generally accepted among those churches which wished to be regarded as orthodox. Other sacred writings survived for other communities, until over time the imperial power enforced conformity. We know, from a considerable body of writings outside the canon, that in different provenances different texts held sway. What the councils eventually achieved was the creation of an orthodox conformity of many churches, but by no means of all churches. Much persecution helped to create the illusion of uniformity, and the arrow of time allowed the mythology of the victors to write the history books.

Even when orthodoxy of a kind had been established in the West, and the canon of Christian scripture had been agreed to by the many constituent churches of Christendom, the determinative factors in the shaping of Christian theology were not biblical as such. The Bible, no doubt, played some part in the development of Christian thought, because many of the churches' theologians produced commentaries on books of the Bible (mostly of the Septuagint version) in which they read the sacred text in the light of their own hermeneutic principles. The gospel story – in various forms because there were numerous Gospels – was important, but within the context of eucharistic communities which had developed non- or post-biblical liturgies. A reading of Origen on the Bible, or of Augustine's *Confessions* or his *City of God*, will certainly demonstrate the importance of scripture for such theologians; but the use of the text is subtle and varied and very much informed by the philosophical holdings of the writers. These prior principles were not biblical. It is this synthesis of philosophical viewpoints and the reading principles of individual writers which constitutes the glory of the early Christian biblical commentators. Undeniably the Bible plays some part in the development of the rich hermeneutical treasury of Christian writings, but it is only a part of a much larger intellectual movement and should not be exaggerated. What created Christian orthodoxy was not the Bible or beliefs about the Bible, but a network of many things including the reception of sacred writings (Septuagint/Vulgate) and the creation of other sacred writings.

It seems to me to be the outstanding Protestant heresy of the Reformation that it elevated the Bible to a position of authority that it had never had before the sixteenth century. This biblicism has subsequently distorted the way many Christians read the history of the churches, by reading back into it views about the Bible which belong more to post-Reformation thought than to earlier Christian notions of scripture. This is not a claim that the Bible was really unimportant before the Reformation. Far from it – but the importance of the Bible before the sixteenth century, especially in the pre-Gutenberg age of printing, is a difficult matter to judge because it was part of a complex web of tradition and magisterium.

A few paragraphs cannot do justice to the assessment of the role of the Bible in the churches, or in the Catholic Church, over the thousand years or so of its existence as a Christian book before the Reformation. The complexities of that role may be checked by the enquiring reader having a look at Origen, Augustine and Jerome on the one hand and Bernard of Clairvaux, Peter Abelard, Thomas Aquinas and Dante on the other hand. When later Protestant polemicists accused the Catholic Church of having developed doctrines and practices which were not to be found in the Bible, they were testifying to the fact that the Bible had not been used in the construction of much Christian teaching. The great formulations of the creeds might have been included in these charges, for if the Bible contributed the sacred story, the theologians had constructed the theology from other sources. From the creation of the world to its ending, with the story of Jesus transformed by theological dogma in the middle, this is what the Bible really provided for the medieval churches. What the reformers seemed to have had in mind (among many other things) was some mythic vision of the past to which they thought the Church should return, and this coincided with views drawn by them from the Bible. In the place of the Church's authority they put the authority of the Bible and, adjusting some of the books of the canon, they set about constructing an alternative magisterium.

The newly emergent world of printing may have contributed to the reformers overrating the Bible by making Bibles more readily available, and the gap between the Bible and Christian theology – the problematic of this book! – certainly afforded them the opportunity of reading the book quite differently. In developing new hermeneutic principles and practices the reformers automatically created a new book, which in turn shaped the emerging religious communities which gave their allegiance to different developing traditions.

But the newer ways of reading the Bible were also symptomatic of the disintegration of the churches. The Bible consists of a collection of writings from the past, and in trying to reform church structures by turning to the past the reformers inevitably donned the mask of the past (to use Karl Marx's criticism of Luther). They attempted to repeat in their own time words from the past, but without adjusting the words for the passage of time, or recognizing that as part of the Catholic Church's possessions the Bible itself was part of the problem. Paul's words in the first century were one thing, but to repeat the same words fifteen centuries later was not to be doing the same thing as Paul was imagined to have been doing. The point being made here was well made by Jorge Luis Borges in his famous story *The Don Quixote of Pierre Menard*. Although the Don Quixote of Pierre Menard is word for word the same as Cervantes's famous novel it is not, because the passage of time has made the great early-seventeenth-century novel part of the culture and the act of copying it out makes Menard's action a different kind of activity. No wonder the reformers failed to reform the Church and just produced more churches. But they had freed the Bible from its older medieval cage and let it loose without a controlling hermeneutic.

Ecclesiastical magisteriums were replicated by the reformers, but there was such a multiplicity of them that by the eighteenth century the distinguishing mark of the Protestant churches was their number rather than anything more significant. Yet out of that freeing of the Bible from the control of the Church, and therefore from its authorizing sources, came the Bible as cultural entity and object for study in itself. This is where the rise of critical theology joins with the spirit of the Enlightenment to free the Bible from ecclesiastical control. The transformations of Christian culture since the Reformation have resulted in contemporary secular society, and in that society the Bible has a precarious position as cultural object. It survives still among the churches as sacred book and, as long as literacy remains widespread in the West, it will survive (in some sense) as a literary object. This has been part of the price of the reformers' activities – in freeing the

71

Bible from the magisterium of the Church they freed it in the long run from religious control. Now it is a book open to whichever prevailing hermeneutical wind will sweep it along. This glorious pluralism of possibilities benefits the critical study of the book as much as it does the most extreme forms of fundamentalist handling of the book – and all the multitudinous positions in between.

Now such a very generalized account of the fortunes of the Bible over nearly two millennia will have to serve as an inadequate background for my concern with 'biblical Christianity'. Open-ended uses of the Bible will necessarily justify religious groups treating the book as independent of all context, as much as they will warrant secular uses of the Bible. Different stances and viewpoints will generate distinctive readings of the Bible, so there can be no a priori objection to how any pressure group reads it. Nor can there be any serious protest about how any religious group interprets it within the privacy of their own community, churches or homes. Where the matter begins to get contentious is with competing readings, or when one reading threatens to force itself on other readings. In other words, when readings become overtly political (the question of the implicitly political nature of any or all readings is too complicated to deal with here) and engage with social ideologies, then the observer who is outside a specific mode of discourse is inevitably sucked into the debate. A text as ideological and as political as the Bible is also makes the debate fraught with the problematical.

The central problem with 'biblical Christianity' as I see it is this: Christianity is a process to which parts of the Bible contributed, but is not itself the product of the Bible. So anything calling itself 'biblical Christianity' is talking about a special kind of construct extrapolated from the Bible and (loosely) identified with the historical phenomenon known as Christianity. It is a special use of the term 'Christianity' and lacks any historical referent. Such a religion derived from a collection of books would be a most curiously artificial thing. When it is remembered that the different versions of the Bible reflect centuries of discrete writings in different languages with a great diversity of viewpoint, it must be imagined that any construct derived from it would be most odd. That is why I have titled this chapter 'the chimera of biblical Christianity'. The chimera was a fabulous beast made up of parts of various animals. The word is also used to describe any grotesque product of the human imagination. What the phrase 'biblical Christianity' actually describes is a fabulous beast – that is, a kind of creature which never existed nor could exist – and a grotesquery of the imagination. It is those things because it tries to construct an ahistorical monster made up of discrete elements drawn from bits of the Bible. In less technical terms it is a kind of 'pick 'n mix' form of bookish religion which tries to cobble together texts from the Bible and to give them a contemporary politicized significance, whilst imagining that it is returning to an original state of affairs which once prevailed in the distant past. It is an attempt to repristinate Christianity without understanding the diverse nature of the earliest churches or the discrete writings constituting the Bible.

From the earliest of Christian writings it is clear that what constitutes the 'genius' of Jewish and Christian readings of scripture and other writings – assuming such distinctions would have been recognized by everybody – is their capacity for transforming the written by various hermeneutical ploys. Reading ancient texts in new and different situations, in the light of distinctive values and experiences, and by means of changing hermeneutical systems, they were able to make old texts yield new meanings. Change the reading framework and you change the meaning of texts. A close reading of the multiple ways in which the early Christian (or Jewish for that matter, if the Talmudic handling of scripture is the focus) writers transformed and applied biblical texts to their own situations, will reveal a very wide range of uses of the Bible. A glance at all the different uses of texts in Matthew 1—2 or in the Letter to the Hebrews will make the point without having to go to all the trouble of reading the Church Fathers (the gendered reference is inescapable). But what is really significant is the practice of transforming texts from what they say to what they mean under different conditions. Reading scripture in the light of what happened to Onias (the murdered priest in the Qumran writings) or to Jesus (the murdered prophet from Nazareth) or to the second temple (razed by the Romans in 70 CE) makes *all* the difference to what scripture means. Occasionally a writer may cite a tag from the Bible for ornamentation purposes or to develop a narratological paraphrase of a biblical story, but generally the writers are concerned with the appropriation of scripture for their own situation. And such assimilation of the text requires transformation in order to bring the text into conjunction with the reader-writer's world.

The transformational interpretation of the Bible is not a contentious issue. Any reader of Qumran literature, the New Testament or the Talmuds can see how it works, even though there are differences in all the writings. The point I am making is this: if the standard Christian techniques for reading the Bible of their time (Septuagint/ Vulgate) were essentially a translation of the ancient writings into contemporary forms, then I would question the *Christian* nature of any return to the scriptures in order to read them in a literalistic fashion. While such a treatment of the Bible might well be justifiable on modern grounds, it would not represent what the early Christians practised as the interpretation of scripture. Of course the matter is more complex than any simple description of it. In the ancient churches there were so many writings that occasionally a literal use of tags from scripture can be found, and in the development of Christendom in the centuries after the great creeds were formulated bits of the Bible were taken literally. But the controlling hermeneutics which regulated the use of scripture were of the allegorical, christological and spiritualizing kind. When therefore people say, 'Let's get back to biblical Christianity,' and start trying to impose a literalistic reading of parts of scripture on other people, I can only assume that they do not know what they are talking about. They are making certain assumptions about the Bible which do not represent the historical development of the Christian communities, but which come from much more recent times. This in itself may be a reasonable approach to make in contemporary society, but it can hardly be put forward as *the* Christian way of reading the Bible. It is a modern Christian reading of scripture, but it is far removed from how the Bible was read in the formative period of Christian exegesis.

The dilemma the emergent Christian imperial power found itself facing when it tried to fund society with ethical standards was created by the serious lack of social ethics in the New Testament. (There are ethics in that volume but they are directed at small groups of Christians living in expectancy of the end of the world or in situations which separated them from the mass of people.) The changing circumstances of imperial Christianity forced the authorities to find ethics which could be applied to society in general, pagan as well as Christian. Here they had to have recourse to their Old Testament, but without the benefit of the Christian transformations of that book. Various arguments had been developed which cleverly reclaimed the Jewish Torah as the means of controlling society. By making a distinction between 'moral' and 'ceremonial' law they were able to enforce the Mosaic law on society. No justification can be found for this differentiation in the text itself and its imposition on the book has raised endless problems to this day.

The fundamental dichotomy introduced into the Pentateuch by Christian reinterpretation of the Bible has constituted one of the most problematical treatments of scripture throughout the history of the Christian reading of the Bible. Having transformed the text by christological allegorization the theologians were forced to return to a literal understanding of *parts* of the Bible. It is not a literal reading of the text which is problematical, but the picking and choosing of bits and pieces of text which suit one's own argument, and the *re*interpretation of the pieces which do not suit, which exposes the inherent weaknesses of the hermeneutic employed. Any fool can reinterpret a text by changing at will what does not fit in order to make the text conform to expectations. This is the hermeneutic of Procrustes. A straight reading of the Mosaic regulations set forth in the books of Exodus to Deuteronomy (the four scrolls of Moses) will reveal the small print of the covenant imposed at Sinai on the people of Israel. These regulations helped to shape the cultus of the second temple period, and in various reinterpreted and enhanced forms contributed to the development of (what is popularly known as) 'orthodox' Judaism. But the Christian transformation of the Bible threw out all such regulations and regarded all expectations in the Bible as having been fulfilled in Jesus. The rituals of the ancient religion were fully replaced by newer ones: baptism for circumcision, eucharist for passover, the death of Jesus in commemorative forms for sacrifice; dietary laws disappeared (those imposed by the meeting of apostles and elders in Acts 15.20 seem not to have survived in practice for any length of time). Yet the lack of serious moral and ethical foundations in the development of Christian communities (the ethics in the New Testament, especially in the epistles, are often Stoic and Roman bourgeoisie forms) would appear to have forced a return to a more serious and non-typological reading of parts of the older Bible.

Centuries of reading the Hebrew Bible *as if* it had been written, if not by then for Christians, predisposes the modern reader to think that the moral-ceremonial division is an obvious way of reading the Mosaic regulations. It is not. So-called moral laws are mixed in with ceremonial regulations and there is nothing in the Exodus-

Deuteronomy material which suggests that parts of it are more important than other parts. Everything is attributed to divine *command* and such commands are not for reinterpreting into suggestions or requests. Of course the commands could be regarded in a different age as being obsolete or superseded by other matters. If that were the case, then copies of the old commands would only have an antiquarian value. It is the holding on to the old writings and their eventual incorporation into a new set of sacred scriptures which makes them so problematic. The Jewish origins of some of the earliest Christian communities entailed the use of the Jewish scriptures, but the widespread development of Christian churches in non-Jewish environments rendered those writings less than useful. Thus the major problem, beyond that of moral-ceremonial selective readings of the text, is the creation and possession of holy books in the first place. There is a cluster of problems here which cannot be explored in this book, but always the real problem comes back time and time again to the Bible itself.

If the Hebrew Bible afforded Christianity with many of its social regulations for governing society (pagan and otherwise), it did so by a most curious amalgam of literal, symbolic and allegorical readings. Sacrifice was no longer imposed on the communities, but the ritual laws of purity were. In the absence of any equivalent social regulations, it may have been inevitable that the communities which began existence as gatherings of people waiting for the end of the world and developed over centuries into the early medieval churches should have created such a mixture of Hebrew, Greek and Roman cultural notions as constituted the Christian religion (in its many forms). The thousand years between the emergence of conciliar Christianity in the West and the Reformation saw the flourishing of Christian Europe and the production of the laws which governed life in Christian society. Since the breakdown of Christian society over the past two centuries (the landmarks in that disintegration may be variously identified in retrospect as the Enlightenment and the emergence of scientific method, the development of thought due to Kant and Hegel, Marx and Darwin, Freud and Einstein, and the revolutionary changes in social processes and secularization since the industrial revolution) there have been many vain attempts to return to the world imagined to have existed when Christianity ruled Europe. As part of such nostalgia I daresay the demands for 'biblical Christianity' have their setting in modern life and are a reaction against the acids of modernity. But the imposition of a selection of biblical regulations on people without any commitment to the Christian religion will only expose further the incoherence of the regulations. Such regulations may work within religious communities, but they cannot be imposed on society in general and especially not in the modern scientific-technological world in which we live. They cannot refuse history to such an extent and survive as coherent principles for constructing modern society.

A close reading of Leviticus will convince any modern reader of the pointlessness of trying to construct society today after the model of such regulations. Perhaps typological manipulations of the text can render the book meaningful for religious communities, but the rules stated in Leviticus belong too much to their own time and culture to be capable of modernization. To ignore the repeated demands for precise sacrificial processes in the text is to admit that the book cannot operate at its natural first-order level of meaning. All subsequent interpretation of it must then be secondary or antiquarian-historical. There are of course some very interesting communal rulings in the book: e.g. 'You shall not oppress your neighbour or rob him'; 'You shall not be partial to the poor or defer to the great'; 'You shall love your neighbour as yourself' (Lev. 19.13, 15, 18). On the same level are other rulings: 'There shall not come upon you a garment of cloth made of two kinds of stuff'; 'Every one who curses his father or mother shall be put to death'; 'If a man lies with a male as with a woman . . . they shall be put to death' (Lev. 19.19; 20.9, 13). It is the totality of the regulations which forms the community and constitutes the keeping of the covenant. Change them, update them, reinterpret them, and they become other than the historical regulations of a people living under the conditions of time and history. Later Jewish and Christian readings of the regulations were forced by circumstances to change how some of those rules applied – the destruction of the second temple made sacrifice impossible so the rules on sacrifice had to be understood in metaphorical and symbolical ways. Time changes everything. Cultures change and the literal readings of ancient texts have to give way to different kinds of readings. Hence any demand for a return to olden times and ways of reading is a refusal of history. It is an attempt to go back to an imagined past by ignoring the passage of time and the inevitable changes brought about by the radical transformations of the recent centuries in European society.

'Biblical Christianity' and sexual ethics

By its very nature this book is a rather generalized account of things, nowhere more so than in this chapter. A specific issue which may serve to exemplify the phenomenon under scrutiny will illustrate the problem very well. The voices which I hear demanding a return to or a re-creation of 'biblical Christianity' seem generally to be united in their opposition to modern sexual mores. In this rejection of the so-called 'sexual revolution' they are certainly in line with traditional Christian values. Since the writings of the New Testament, one of the few constants in Christian traditions has been the asexuality of Christian virtue. Christian values, until the twentieth century, have generally rejected any form of sexual practice and have made virginity and chastity the great virtues of Christian behaviour. Other Christian communities which did not develop into the mainstream of conciliar religion may have had other values and practices, but what became Christianity for European society always made sexual practice a marginal activity of Christian virtue and confined it to the family. The roots of asexual virtue are to be found in the New Testament but nowhere in the Hebrew Bible. Among the many great contrasts between the sacred writings of the Jews and those created by the Christians, one of the most striking is that between the embracing of the sexual in the Hebrew Bible (the Song of Songs is only the most obvious example) and its refusal in the New Testament (Paul's allowance of sexual practice in 1 Corinthians 7.9 hardly makes it a Christian virtue).

There were no doubt many reasons for the radically different values placed on sex and family relations by Jews and Christians. Running through the Gospels is the theme of the Christian communities as alternative families (e.g. Matt. 12.46–50) and the notion of relationship to Jesus as destructive of familial relations (e.g. Matt. 10.34–37). Stoic notions of celibacy and other influences favouring ascetic rejection of sexual engagement no doubt contributed to the development of the Christian asexual ethics which shaped mainstream theology. After the failure of the end of the world expectations (the delay of the *parousia*) and with the emergence of imperial Christianity, the inevitable family relations of most Christians had to be regulated by material taken from the Hebrew

Bible. But the levitical rules had been designed to maintain the purity of a small nation and so were not entirely suitable for regulating large-scale societies. Also, their concern with purity and danger meant that incorporating them into Christian social formation cut across the earlier Christian movement away from purity concerns typified by the Gospel representations of Jesus.

The world of sexual ethics represented by the Hebrew Bible reflects an aggressively reproductive heterosexual one in which any form of deviation from that norm was denounced as an abomination and made liable to the death penalty. Behind these regulations may have been cultic struggles with alternative cultures, and the wholesale banning of practices characteristic of other cults gave to the Jerusalem cultus much of its identifying particularity (*Kulturkampf* is so much the subtext of the Hebrew Bible that it is unlikely to be absent from the Leviticus text). The extent to which the ban on homosexual behaviour in the Hebrew Bible reflects only cultic matters and not also what prevailed among the general populace of the second temple period cannot be determined, because reliable historical information is not available for that period. What the Bible (either testament and any version) represents is not what ancient peoples thought and did but what élites among ancient peoples wrote and tried (perhaps successfully) to impose by way of ideological control. There is no point in translating statements in the Bible to mean 'This is what the ancient Israelites or early Christians thought,' because we do not know enough (or anything much) about the time and conditions of the production of biblical writings to be able to make such judgements. For all we know, everything in the Bible may represent nothing more than the opinions of the writers and the interests they represented. It is therefore impossible to assess whether homosexual practices were common or unusual among Jews in the second temple period. Given the emphases on heterosexual, even incestuous, relations in the Hebrew Bible, and the subsequent developments of familial life in the Judaisms of the Common Era, it is quite likely that homosexual behaviour was no higher than in any other comparable ancient society. But we do not know.

Apart from Paul's paean to the wrath of God in Romans 1, which includes some remarks about the deity having given women and men over to dishonourable passions and unnatural relations, the New Testament has nothing to say about homosexuality (cf. 1 Cor. 6.9, 1 Tim. 1.10). As the book never advocates heterosexual behaviour it may safely be assumed that it would be equally against any practical expression of homosexual activity. The Gospels are absolutely silent on the subject, though there is some advocacy of celibacy as preferable to marriage (the saying about self-emasculation in Matthew 19.12 is tricky). Divorce is forbidden (Matt. 5.32; 19.3–9), though the exception clause suggests a rethinking of the absoluteness of that prohibition. Here the Gospels are more in line with Qumran than with the Hebrew Bible, and any religious structure which embraces both testaments will have problems with the simple contradiction. If the rewriting of the older testament by reinterpretation is accepted as a principle – as it is attributed to Jesus it is difficult to see how people who treat the New Testament as normative can reject it – then it is clear that statements in the Hebrew Bible are not binding on Christians. All the transformations of the Bible in the New Testament, especially in the Gospels, indicate that the earliest Christian communities did not take over the Jewish scriptures without thoroughly rewriting them by reinterpretation. It is the transformed scriptures which were authoritative for some Christian churches. Marriage for Paul is permissive but not an ideal. Some of the smaller writings in the New Testament use marriage as a metaphor of the relationship between Christ and the Church. Otherwise the New Testament has nothing to say on behalf of sexual expression as a positive virtue for Christian people. So if Christians feel they must express themselves sexually, they do so outside their Christian faith.

The uniform hostility to sexual behaviour in so many forms of the Christian religion sits very uneasily with modern bourgeois values associating the family with Christianity. It is not simply a case of mainstream Christian movements having always been against all expressions of homosexual behaviour; they have always been against heterosexual behaviour too. Of course, in the Christian imperium when it proved impossible to get every Christian to be chaste, concessions had to be made to marriage customs, but always in terms of reproduction. Christian marriage may be regarded today by religious people as an ideal, an absolute to be aspired to by every Christian couple, but that is a very modern concept. Classical forms of Christian thinking never made marriage a Christian ideal in any sense. Necessary for the masses and for those who could not live up to Christian ideals perhaps, but never a means whereby Christian virtue could be expressed. The interpretation of the commandment

'You shall not commit adultery' (I cannot call it the seventh commandment because Catholics and Protestants even number the commandments differently!) from Ambrose to Calvin and to a recent Pope, includes the definition of adultery as over-eager sex with one's wife! Sexuality has always been a subject for fear and loathing among orthodox Christian thinkers. So I would not be very much impressed by modern claims that Christianity has always been against homosexuality and that therefore anti-homosexuality should be a desideratum of contemporary Christian values.

Neither Leviticus nor Paul can be regarded as adequate authorities for constructing a modern account of sexuality or sexual relations. Leviticus is too far removed from modernity to be relevant and cannot be recontextualized to contribute usefully to the modern debate. Besides which, the Jewish scriptures having been transformed by New Testament reinterpretation, they are not available to Christians at a literal level of understanding. Taking Leviticus seriously as a historical text has no bearing on contemporary existence, and taking it prescriptively makes for nonsense. Who among the anti-homosexual brigade has not worn garments 'made of two kinds of stuff' (Lev. 19.19) – check the labels on your Marks and Spencer's clothing! Such impurity is on the same level as bestiality and homosexuality and incest. Here I suspect the determinative factors are cultural and aesthetic. When selectivity is at play we pick the laws we approve of and ignore the ones which do not appeal to us. Leviticus makes good ammunition for 'queer-bashing', and such anti-social hostility as is involved in attacking other people's ways of life can always be sweetened with a biblical text. That does not make the practice any the less disgraceful. The ideology of power masked by a biblical quotation remains an expression of power attempting to control others. But in the contemporary debate about sexual identity and the rights of all individuals within a democracy, the use of outmoded texts from Leviticus becomes a modern form of abomination itself.

The prescriptive nature of the Bible

Whether Paul is an adequate authority on the subject of how human beings express themselves sexually may be more debatable in Christian circles. Jewish writings such as Leviticus may legitimately

81

be left to Jews to interpret as they see fit in the modern world; but do the writings of the New Testament have any prescriptive hold on Christian communities today? That is the larger setting for enquiring about the value for our day of Paul's opinions on the sexual behaviour of women and men in the Rome of his day. While Paul's reading of the sexual mores of his time is a very interesting application of the notion of causality sometimes found among the biblical prophets (cf. Isa. 3.1–5), it is so tied into his general argument in Romans that it must be regarded as a highly tendentious interpretation of social reality designed to underwrite the theology of his letter. As a statement of Christian thinking the Epistle to the Romans may be a brilliant piece of rhetorical argumentation – both Luther and Barth stumbled over it and fell – but it is neither a comprehensive statement of prescriptive thought nor is it the only voice in the New Testament. It is just one of the many voices speaking in that collection of books and must not be read as if it were the *summa* of early Christian thinking. It is one man's opinion and, although the Marcionite heresy of overvaluing Paul has been a virus in many Christian readings of scripture, must be judged accordingly. The long history of Christian persecution of homosexual people cannot be justified on the strength of such a slender piece of opinionation. Nor can that long history of prejudice be used as constitutive of normative teaching, because the history of Christian antisemitism is equally as long and nobody today would regard it as warranted still by such wont and custom (see Chapter Four).

The prescriptive nature of the Bible is a subject which neatly divides traditional and critical attitudes towards it. Demands for a return to or a development of 'biblical Christianity' stem from circles committed to traditional dogmas of biblical inspiration and confessional modes of discourse. For them the Bible – or to be more precise *beliefs about* the Bible – is prescriptive by definition, even though this is not a historical Christian position. How can the Bible be the sole authority for Christian communities? It was not such in the earliest centuries when the communities were emerging in the Roman empire, and no amount of citations about sacred writings extrapolated from the New Testament (e.g. 2 Tim. 3.16) says a thing about the New Testament itself. Its authority is derived from decisions made by the churches in the fourth century and that factor cannot be gainsaid. The system of beliefs held to represent orthodox Christianity includes some things which are not to be found in the

New Testament and other things which are enhanced developments of biblical ideas under the influence of later non-biblical thought. Who would be able to construct the doctrine of the Holy Trinity from scripture alone? Yet trinitarian belief is the most fundamental element in orthodox thought. Who could possibly reach from the synoptic Gospels the conclusion that Jesus of Nazareth was the second person of that Holy Trinity? Or read the prologue to the Fourth Gospel as evidence of trinitarian thought? Who could imagine the Jesus of the Gospels founding the Holy Catholic Church?

These questions – rhetorical and otherwise – are the mere beginnings of the exposure of the inadequacy of the New Testament for Christian theology if orthodox Christian belief is to be the starting point of the discussion. Nobody could be an orthodox Christian on the strength of the New Testament alone. As has already been stressed, such orthodoxy is a complex amalgam of beliefs and practices derived from centuries of Christian existence and utilizing some elements in the New Testament. But many features of the New Testament developed in other ways and many Christian communities were not represented by the creation of orthodoxy. Many Christians with alternative beliefs were butchered by other Christians in the centuries after the emergence of orthodox thought. These complexities are easily ignored by the orthodox but cannot be glossed over by the historian or scholar. Gnostic gospels may have no appeal to the orthodox, but to the critical scholar they are very important documents about Christian communities of long ago who did not share in the triumph of orthodoxy. To read the many patristic writers and to discover the variety of Christian thought which once flourished in the name of Christ is an invitation to exercise the hermeneutics of suspicion on the reception of orthodox mythology.

Many important issues are clustered together here. Questions about the development of Christian dogma and the nature of heresy, enquiries about authority and Christian formation (or deformation as the case may be), puzzlement about lost communities and abandoned scriptures. Too many questions to pick up here, but all bearing on why the critical reading of the Bible must reject as chimerical the notion of 'biblical Christianity'.

The big question about the relationship between the Bible and the development of Christian dogma is a variation on the question of development which John Henry Newman addressed in his famous *Essay on the Development of Christian Doctrine* (1845). Newman showed to his own satisfaction that all was well with the conviction that the teaching of Christ and his apostles was the same as that taught by the Catholic Church through all the centuries of its existence. Such a sanguine conclusion was but the premiss with which he started, so it is not surprising that he arrived at the destination he set out for. Whatever criticisms may be made against Newman's essay it must be recognized that at least he was worrying about an important issue. Does development entail continuity or discontinuity? If there are breaks and changes in what is developed, then in what sense can that development be identified with the past? Yet the New Testament is too diverse in its teachings and too inchoate for any one development to be identified with the totality of the collection of writings. From the writings constituting the New Testament many different doctrines and practices may be developed. Consider the role of women in the early churches, especially in the Gospels. There is a high visibility of women in the New Testament, which disappears from the orthodox church structures of later centuries (though one discovers that they were very important in the development of other churches and at various times in ecclesiastical history).

The question of women is too big to handle here, and yet reading the Bible today in a critical mode cannot avoid encountering that question. Like much else discussed in this book it illustrates well the relationship between texts and the situational context in which they are read. I am not here concerned with modern silly questions about the ordination of women – I say silly because the traditional answers to the questions which assert that 'Jesus never ordained women to be priests' trivialize the argument. Jesus, according to the canonical Gospels, never ordained anyone to be a priest. Such roles belong to later social developments. The question of women in the churches (or in society today) is too important for this kind of textual reading. This is not how texts should be read. It makes for a trivialization of texts as if they could function as proof-texts for future generations.

I know that the Bible was used as a quarry for carving out proof-texts in post-Reformation thought, but sensibilities have changed greatly since then. A modern reading of *The Westminster Confession of Faith* is virtually impossible for anybody other than devotees and historians, because the proof-texts used in that massive volume are so ornamental and conventional rather than substantive and argumentative. They are the silliness of another age. Whether it is the

Bible or the Confessions of the Reformed churches, each document or collection of documents represents the production of its time and culture. As such they have to be read in historical terms and not as permanently prescriptive for all time.

While advocates of 'biblical Christianity' will disagree with this diagnosis of texts because they regard the Bible with non-biblical theories, I begin to wonder whether such an infantile attitude towards the Bible does not raise the important question of whether the churches were wise or Christian in creating Christian scriptures in the first place. Two questions are here really: the one about the wisdom of creating the Christian Bible and one which may be asked about my describing 'biblical Christianity' as infantile. The easier question first: I describe as infantilism the vain quest to go back to an imaginary beginning in order to start all over again and to go on starting all over again. It is infantile because it is an attempt to ignore eighteen hundred years of development in order to construct an ahistorical entity imagined to have existed once before in the past. It is as if a grown person were to revert to babyhood again. Even if the mythical beginning had had a historical actuality, it would not be possible to return to it now. Post-Christian Europe is not virgin territory waiting for Christian missionaries, it is very much the product of Christianity among other things, and this is what nearly two millennia of Christian beliefs and practices look like. The Don Cupitts and David Jenkinses are as much the product of the Christian churches as are the Billy Grahams and Jerry Falwells. To imagine that the solutions to being an adult are to be found in returning to babyhood is to be infantile in every sense of the word.

The other question about the creation of Christian scripture is much more difficult to answer. While it may be a matter of great regret that the development of the churches included the Jewish practice of creating sacred scriptures – what some of the reformers might have called 'judaizing' – nothing can be done about it now. For fifteen hundred years the Christian Bible has been in existence and it cannot be wished out of existence – that would be an infantile wish! Marcion's rejection of the Hebrew Bible and his reduced collection of Christian writings (whether he knew more and rejected them or did not know what later became canonical writings is an open question) indicates an awareness of the problem of possessing ideologically unsuitable books. While the dominant opinion of orthodoxy has favoured an expanded collection of writings –

modified by the reformers for their churches – the question, very much Christopher Evans's territory (see Bibliographical Notes), is well worth pondering.

As I understand the 'biblical Christianity' movement, it seems to operate with the principle *extra textum nulla salus* 'there is no salvation outside the text' – a modern equivalent of the much older Catholic principle of there being no salvation outside the Church. It also works with the belief that there are patterns of a prescriptive nature in the New Testament. A critical reading of that collection will fail to find any patterns in it and the degree of prescriptiveness in it is a variable according to how individual sections are read. There is no doubt that many post-Reformation churches have made the New Testament prescriptive. In practice that means that a few selective portions are prescribed and the rest read according to hermeneutical principles developed by the various churches. All of these beliefs and practices amount to a kind of divinization of the Bible – its return to being a magical book – so it is hardly surprising that I find the quest for such an entity as being chimerical. In my opinion the quest represents such a failure to grasp the historical nature of the books of the Bible (the version is unimportant), or to understand how the books have been used over many centuries of Christian activity, that it must be regarded as a movement doomed to failure.

That does not mean that it will not be a very popular movement. I daresay it may appeal to thousands of religious people. But the incoherence of the beliefs will militate against it just as proved to be the case in the nineteenth-century Scottish Free Church, where biblical criticism made the strongest inroads in what were theologically the most conservative of churches. Any responsible reading of the Bible today must make the reader question inherited beliefs about the book. It requires little criticality to read about slavery, cruelty in the name of God, antisemitism and prejudice in the scriptures and not be made aware of gaps between the text and modern values. In such ways the Bible deconstructs itself for the modern reader. A reading of the history of the reception of the Bible will demonstrate the truth of Mark Twain's analysis (see the first epigraph to this chapter) of how time and practice have corrected the Bible while retaining the text.

The political nature of the 'biblical Christianity' pressure groups will expose the tensions between what they believe about the Bible and what the book says – all those death camps which would have to be constructed to impose the levitical regulations about sexual practices! As Matthew Arnold says in discussing the folly of juxtaposing science and dogmatic religion – how prophetic he was in many ways! – 'Nothing but shocks and collisions can come.' I have applied that saying to a different juxtaposition, that of the Bible and modern society. It is fine to read and practise the Bible in the privacy of the religious group, but to attempt to impose bits of it on society is folly. It is to imagine that there have been no real changes in the past few centuries and that the modern world is just the ancient world in modern dress. Such poor social analysis – or dogmatic belief to be more accurate – will never succeed in grasping the nature of how things are today.

This reactionary use of the Bible makes one sympathize with van Gogh's determination to walk away from a certain kind of dead religion in order to devote himself to a better way (his art) of finding joy. Who can forget that painting of his in which the huge formal Bible rigidly dominates the picture in contrast to the tiny much-used copy of Emile Zola's *La Joie de Vivre*? His juxtaposition of the rigidity of formal dogma and the flexibility (user-friendly) of the pleasures of 'real life' is a brilliant statement of a truth often lost sight of by the biblicist. The Bible, if it is imposed on people in all the wrong ways, can be and is an instrument of death – the letter which kills, to use Paul's phrase – in contrast to the life of nature and experience. It does not take an art critic or a connoisseur of painting to observe the sharp distinction between the paintings done by Vincent van Gogh when he lived in the rectory in the Netherlands and those produced by him when he discovered the sun and light of the French impressionists and the south of France. Small wonder that van Gogh should have asked the question, 'Is the Bible enough for us?' and then answered it with a well-known quotation from the New Testament resurrection stories: 'Why do you seek the living among the dead?'

The worship of the beast – the chimera of 'biblical Christianity' – appears to be a growing phenomenon of our time. As political structures lurch to the right it is inevitable that social religion will follow. If fundamentalistic attitudes towards and uses of sacred writings (whatever the term 'fundamentalism' may be understood to mean) are on the increase, then we are due to have a great deal more of biblicism in the West. Perhaps we should all be good Marxists and go with the flow of history; but the pendulum will swing back in a time to come and leave fundamentalist readings of the Bible on the dunghills of history. Such readings will break down under their own incoherence and internal contradictions, but not before they have spoiled many lives and rendered the Bible unspeakable for generations of sensitive people. The chimera can only be hunted, I suspect, by the imagination and great good humour in the service of reason and intelligence.

4
The People of the Jews

Is the desolation of the land the result of the fatal embrace of the Deity? Hapless are the favorites of heaven.

Herman Melville

·Jew, for you the homeless fruit of
aggressive silence.

So, with God dead, I found my Jewishness confirmed in the book, at the predestined spot when it came upon its face, the saddest, most unconsoled that man can have.
Because being Jewish means exiling yourself in the word and, at the same time, weeping for your exile.
The return to the book is a return to forgotten sites.

Edmond Jabès

Odour of blood when Christ was slain
Made all Platonic tolerance vain

William Butler Yeats

Qoheleth's opinion on the fortunes of humankind was that time and chance happen to everybody (Eccles. 9.11). He might have added 'and to things as well'. Time especially happens to everybody and to everything and it is seldom kind. Through time the Bible has undergone many transformations and transmogrifications. It certainly is not exempt from the process of history. Now how it has been handled and interpreted through time are immense subjects for discussion and well beyond the scope of this book. Equally formidable are the effects time has had on it, changing its meaning and significance in so many different ways that no single interpreter could possibly chart them all. Whether it is Jerry Falwell *autographing* copies of the Bible or the Argentinian footballer Diego Maradona giving a new meaning to the biblical phrase 'the hand of God', time transforms everything, even the Bible. The new uses may be serious or silly, ironic or straightforward, useful or dangerous, ornamental or ethical, foreseeable or novel. Who can predict or anticipate what new meanings will be given to biblical words, phrases, passages and books? Who can guess the ways the Bible will be used in contexts yet unknown? For that matter who could delineate the ways in which the Bible (or parts of it) has been used in the past? It is used in courts of law for people to swear on, it has been smuggled into pre-*glasnost* communist countries, it regularly features as a weapon of protest against ecumenical Christians, textual references are superstitiously advertised at World Cup football matches, unreadably printed extracts from it are stuffed as tracts into the hands of puzzled pedestrians in the shopping malls of the West, and some religious people prize it as 'the most valuable thing that Earth possesses'. Many of these examples suggest an element of farce, and remind one of Karl Marx's gloss on Hegel's observation about how facts and persons of great importance in world history occur as it were twice: the first time as tragedy, the second as farce. The Bible has been too protean in its long history to be limited to the tragic and the farcical, but those marxian poles are worth bearing in mind when contemplating the history of the interpretation of the Bible.

The Jews in the New Testament

In this chapter I wish to look at one specific topic arising out of the Bible which will illustrate a further dimension of the problem constituted by the Bible for theology. In this case my concern will be with a biblical *topos* (a commonplace) in the light of the subsequent history of the referent of that *topos*. Text and history (*traditum* and *traditio* to use technical language) interact in such a way that it is not possible to read the *topos* in the Bible without instantly being put in mind of the afterlife (*Nachleben*) of the text. My *topos* is the Jews in the New Testament; and the very phrase 'the Jews' is a metonym for the long history of Christian antisemitism, starting in the New Testament and going on down the centuries until in the twentieth century it spawned the death camps of Nazi Germany. This chapter's title is a phrase which appears in Acts 12.11 where reference is made to 'the people of the Jews'. It is a curious phrase, and unusual in the

New Testament where the normal expression would be 'the Jews'. I use it in this book because reading it in Acts, in the general context of the New Testament, it has resonances for any modern reader who is at all familiar with the fate of the Jews in Christendom. In the beginning is the end!

The late medieval painter Matthias Grünewald created a great altarpiece at Isenheim in the early sixteenth century. It has become justifiably famous and consists of nine panels depicting the nativity of the Christ child, numerous pictures of saints and patrons and a brutal representation of the crucifixion. In the nativity scene there is a consort of angels on the left and on the right the adoring mother holds the child in her arms. At her feet is a chamberpot. A close scrutiny of that object will reveal that it is decorated with a frieze of Hebrew letters. This writing indicates that the chamberpot represents the Jews. It is a statement about the pollution constituted by the Jews. The Jews are a piss pot. Such a representation of the Jews followed the standard code of Grünewald's day – the use of Hebrew letters to indicate the Jews or to symbolize their presence can be seen in many paintings before his time and in many woodcuts of the period. Such depictions of the Jews as unclean objects, pollutants of good Christian society, or as worshippers of the Devil, or as killers of Christ, or as devotees of sows (the infamous *Judensau*), or as murderers of Christian children in blood rituals relating to the Jewish passover, were so common in the medieval period that Grünewald's chamberpot is really quite unremarkable. I suspect that many viewers of that great altarpiece will never have noticed it.

The pictures and woodcuts of the fifteenth and sixteenth centuries will bear much scrutiny by the sensitive lover of art and religion. They are a lasting testimony to what was part and parcel of everyday life in Christendom. For many centuries good Christian folk had despised and loathed the Jews. Few opportunities were missed for making life miserable for them. Since the end of the eleventh century, when the first crusade took place, there had been pogroms against Jews. Technically the word 'pogrom' comes from Russian via Yiddish, and describes organized persecution of the Jews in nineteenth-century Russia. But the massacre denoted by the word is much older than the time of Czarist Russia. Massacring the Jews was part of the crusading spirit which swept Christian Europe from the eleventh to the thirteenth century.

Incidentally, the term 'crusade' is an interesting example of how words develop and transform original meanings into ironic reflections of those meanings. Derived, via various languages, from the Latin word *crux*, 'cross', and influenced by the Spanish word *cruzada* (from *cruzar* 'to take up the cross'), it is a word which once denoted that Roman gibbet used to execute criminals and Jews became identified with a term meaning to pursue a holy war against the Muslims living in the Holy Land. The symbol of salvation became a symbol of destruction. A similar deterioration of language can be seen in the Nazi transformation of a religious symbol into the *swastika* (*Hakenkreuz*). Under the banner of the cross Christians marched across Europe massacring Jews on the way to massacre Muslims in order to regain the holy places associated with Christian origins in the Holy Land. In the name of Christ, the giver of life, they brought death to many. Hence Jews and Muslims have been very wary of Christians and their symbols of life and universal love.

There is such a long history of Christian antisemitism over nineteen centuries, and much of it is fairly well-known, that I do not intend to depress the reader with another cataloguing of the horrors and atrocities imposed by the Christian churches on the Jews. My real concern is with the roots of this antisemitism in the Bible and with the problems of reading the New Testament today in the light of that appalling history. This seems to me to be a very important element in the problem of the Bible for Christian theology. It also bears very much on the problem of how texts are to be read, especially in the light of their history. Can what is outside the text really be ignored when reading a text? What is, and what is not, outside a text?

The word 'Jew' comes from the Hebrew for Judah and describes those people who lived in the territory of Judah (i.e. Judeans), especially in the period of the second temple (Persian and Graeco-Roman periods – the more usual term 'postexilic' is avoided here because it has unwarranted ideological overtones to it). The word is found in the Hebrew Bible mostly in the book of Esther, but it also appears in Jeremiah and Ezra-Nehemiah. In the New Testament it is especially used in the books of John and Acts as a plural – 'the Jews' – and describes the Jewish people or nation. While it also occurs in a number of other New Testament writings – the three Synoptic Gospels use it infrequently – its statistical distribution in the Fourth Gospel and Acts is highly significant.

A close reading of all the occurrences of references to 'the Jews' in these two sources will demonstrate certain patterns of use. Apart from the Jews who were sympathetic towards or who became Christians in Acts and a few general references to Jews in John, the most dominant pattern which emerges is one of great hostility and viciousness on the part of the Jews towards Jesus and then towards his earliest followers. A simple reading of the role of the Jews in the seizure, trial and execution of Jesus in John 18—19 is revealing. Jesus would never have been murdered by the Roman authority if it had not been for the insistence of the Jews that Pontius Pilate should show no weakness or liberality but should do his duty and execute Jesus. In Acts, the Jews who did not convert to the new movement are a constant source of trouble and persecution for the Christians. The context of my epigraphic source in Acts 12 is a good example of this standard depiction of the Jews. In the story about his arrest and imprisonment, Peter speaks the words which contain the ominous phrase 'the people of the Jews'. This story is contained within the larger context of stories about Herod the king and is a reflection of the Jewish pleasure at Herod's murder of James the brother of John.

> About that time Herod the king laid violent hands upon some who belonged to the church. He killed James the brother of John with the sword; *and when he saw that it pleased the Jews*, he proceeded to arrest Peter also. (Acts 12.1–3 *emphases added*)

Here the Jews – not some or a few or certain Jews but *the Jews* (*die Juden* as a later culture would express the same sentiment) – are represented as one of the forces encouraging Herod in one of his periodic bouts of aggression (in the New Testament generally the name 'Herod' is a symbol of murderous passions). Whether Herod, like Pontius Pilate in a different context, needed any such responsive support from the Jews is neither here nor there. In the story of Peter's imprisonment the Jews are to blame and the angelic intervention which rescues Peter does so 'from the hand of Herod *and from all that the people of the Jews were expecting*' (verse 11). But for that angel the Jews would have been guilty of yet another murder of a Christian!

I do not think it necessary to go through every story in the Fourth Gospel or in the book of Acts which deals with plots by the Jews against Jesus, the Christians or Paul in order to make the point. As represented by Acts (was the author of the third Gospel the same person who wrote Acts?) the Jews are a regular source of plots against the Christians, especially against Paul (e.g. Acts 20.3; 23.12). At times distinctions are made between different groups of Jews (e.g. Pharisees and Sadducees as in Acts 23.6–10), but generally such subtleties are avoided. Jews are not always represented as being hostile to Paul; on occasion in prolonged debate between him and them there are different and rational reactions (cf. Acts 28.23–25). But the overall impression one gets from reading Acts is that of enormous hostility on the part of the Jews against the Christians, and the book ends on a note of direct criticism of the Jews using the words of Isaiah (Acts 28.25–28 citing the Septuagint version of Isa. 6.9–10). The Jews really frustrated all the preaching efforts of the early Christian movement and forced some of the preachers to abandon the Jews in favour of preaching to the Gentiles (i.e. the non-Jewish world).

The stories are told, of course, from the Christian viewpoint. We do not possess the other side of the stories. The Jewish voice is never heard. So the honest reader of these stories cannot make any judgement about their historicity or authenticity. They are, like so much else in whatever version of the Bible is favoured, propaganda for a particular viewpoint and a one-sided account of things. The official history of the beginnings of the churches as represented by the book of Acts tells the story from a strongly anti-Jewish viewpoint. That account will become with the passage of time part of the Christian canon of sacred scripture and this appalling (mis)representation of *the Jews* will be the Christian image of the Jew heard by millions of Christians down through the ages. Whatever subtler depictions of Jews or Israel are to be found elsewhere in the New Testament (e.g. Rom. 9—11) – for the book is certainly nothing like a collection of unified beliefs but is a highly diversified amalgam of very different viewpoints – they will prove incapable of combating the representation of Jews in the development of the churches in Acts, or the Fourth Gospel's hostile presentation of them as the enemies of Jesus.

Though at times in John the text can be quite confusing in its references to the Jews, the underlying value judgments made about them are clear. Try reading John 8. Its tricky interweaving of stories and discourses about Jesus and the Jews makes it very difficult to follow who is what in the account. Teaching in the temple (the other Gospels tend to keep Jesus out of Jerusalem until a few days before his death), Jesus has many conversations with the Jews, but the identity of the Jews fluctuates as the discourses unfold. Speaking to 'the Jews *who had believed in him*' (v. 31) Jesus eventually says, 'You are of your father the devil, and your will is to do your father's desires' (v. 44). Surely some mistake here! Should not this be said to the Jews who had *not* believed in Jesus rather than to his Jewish followers? But of course in the Fourth Gospel the real *topos* is 'the Jews', and subtle distinctions such as 'Jews who believed in Jesus' are quickly subsumed in the dominant theme.

What is most important about John 8 is that statement about the devil being the father of the Jews. That charge will be remembered for many, many centuries and will be translated into woodcuts and depictions of the Jews worshipping the Devil – now grown to Gothic proportions under the careful fertilization of medieval theology – as their natural father. All subsequent controversies between Jews and Christians can be read as variations on John 8. The words of the canonical writings are awesome in the way they prefigure nearly two thousand years of relations between the churches and the synagogues (I use those two terms in the loosest sense possible – as metonyms). They are worth repeating here just to underline the terms of the debate and to catch the subtext of the discussion:

> Jesus said to them, 'If God were your Father, you would love me, for I proceeded and came forth from God; I came not of my own accord, but he sent me. Why do you not understand what I say? It is because you cannot bear to hear my word. *You are of your father the devil*, and your will is to do your father's desires. He was a murderer from the beginning, and has nothing to do with the truth, because there is no truth in him. When he lies, he speaks according to his own nature, for he is a liar and the father of lies. But, because I tell the truth, you do not believe me. Which of you convicts me of sin? If I tell the truth, why do you not believe me? He who is of God hears the words of God; the reason why you do not hear them is that you are not of God.' (John 8.42–47)

Read in the light of Christian antisemitism down through the ages, the words reverberate with frightening intensity and identify the location of the roots of that antisemitism as being in the New Testament itself.

The Fourth Gospel's representation of the Jews is a notorious contribution to the heart and sinews of Christian antisemitism. Though the writer of that book may be accused of depicting the Jews in various pejorative ways, his (I shall assume for the sake of convenience and in order to avoid having to write ten pages by way of explanation, that the New Testament writers were male; I have no direct evidence for this assumption) placement of many of his values in the mouth of Jesus makes Jesus the source of antisemitism. While a modern critical reader of the Bible can escape the necessary implications of this mode of narration, the average or 'orthodox' Christian cannot avoid the conclusion that the root of the problem of antisemitism is the words of Jesus.

The Fourth Gospel presents special problems in gospel criticism because it is so different from the other three Gospels, and whatever community it may be the product of may also have been quite distinctive among the early Christian communities. Its discourses and narratives are peculiarly hostile to the Jews and such hostility is not nearly so developed in the other three Gospels.But it should not be assumed that only the Fourth Gospel represents an antisemitic voice. The other Gospels also present the Jews as the enemy of Jesus and as the ones responsible for his murder. The passion narratives tell the story of the death of Jesus in terms of a reluctant Roman governor who was persuaded or manipulated by the Jews in the matter of the actual execution of Jesus. Reading the story one gets the impression that had it not been for the Jews – various strata are identified as 'chief priests', 'elders', 'scribes', 'the whole council', 'the rulers', and occasionally 'the people' (e.g. Luke 23.13) – Jesus would never have been sentenced to death by that kindly Roman governor. Pontius Pilate did everything he could to prevent the execution of Jesus, but such pressure was put on him by the Jewish authorities that he had to yield to their demands and send Jesus to his death by crucifixion. In the Fourth Gospel the pressure comes from 'the Jews' (e.g. John 19.7, 12, 14–16), but all the passion narratives agree on identifying the social group behind the murder of Jesus. The most famous words on this point come not from John's Gospel but from Matthew's:

> So when Pilate saw that he was gaining nothing, but rather that a riot was beginning, he took water and washed his hands before the crowd, saying, 'I am innocent of this man's blood; see to it yourselves.' And *all the people answered*, '*His blood be on us, and on our children!*' (Matt. 27.24–25)

Those words attributed to 'all the people' would echo down through the ages and would be heard again and again wherever Jews were being done to death. And in the twentieth century they would find their grim echoes resounding in the death camps of Auschwitz and hundreds of other places.

Admittedly, there would be other factors of a social and ideological nature that would help to determine the fortunes and fates of specific Jewish communities. I am not saying that a simple, straightforward reading of the Gospels made Christians rush out into the street in order to massacre Jews. It is more complex than that. The prevailing fortunes of different communities in the Roman empire were important elements in whether Jewish and Christian groups were in conflict or at peace with one another. In many parts of Christendom there were no Jewish communities, so persecution never arose. In other parts economic and social considerations determined the relationship. But the great councils from the fourth century onwards (till at least the Council of Trent in the sixteenth century) passed many laws against the Jews and made life among Christian communities rather unpleasant for them. Where Christians had power Jews suffered, where Christians were powerless Jews were better off. After the emergence of the crusading spirit massacres of Jews became a feature of Christian Europe. Yet in spite of all the laws against Jews, and despite the persecutions and Easter massacres, there does not appear to have ever been a sustained policy of exterminating Jews from Christian society. There were many campaigns to convert them to Christian belief and practice, often involving enforced conversion, but even the converted Jews remained second-class citizens. Throughout its history Christian ideology could never tolerate the Jew *as* Jew. The roots of that intolerance are to be found in the New Testament and especially in the Fourth Gospel's formulation of the problem.

Reading John 8 in the light of Jewish-Christian relations since the production of the Gospels makes the text almost prophetic in its representation of the quarrel. The Jews are accused of being the children of their father the devil. The devil is characterized as a liar and murderer and therefore the children by implication are liars and murderers. They will murder Christ by the end of the Gospel, a murder which is represented as being inspired by Satan (John 13.27; cf. Luke 22.3), and throughout the story will refuse to believe in him. Murder, lies, unbelief, diabolical affiliations: all features of the medieval mythology of the Jew in Christian society.

Even the betrayer of Jesus is singled out in a special way. The very

97

name Judas is but a form of the name 'Jew'. Who else but the Jew would betray Jesus into the hands of the authorities? Of all the different disciples, why should the one with the simple name of Jew/Judas be the betrayer? How could it be otherwise! In the dramatic mythology of the passion narrative, the story is concerned with symbols and eternal verities. It is not the mere description of things which happened in the past – history is the least of its concerns. The narrative (and all four Gospels are dominated by the passion story) is cosmic in its dimensions, and the role played by the Jews makes them representative of the dark underside of all that is in opposition to God (i.e. the diabolical). That is how the story will be read for centuries by generations of Christian churches and its genesis is in the canonical Gospels. Its truth will be demonstrated through time by the fact that all Jewish communities persist in their refusal to believe in Jesus the messiah. Belief in Jesus as the messiah is the whole point of the Fourth Gospel (20.31) and also the very turning point between Jew and Christian. So the persistence of the Jewish rejection of Jesus through time confirmed the analysis of John 8 that the Jews were of the devil.

Anti-semitism in conciliar Christianity

When conciliar Christianity began to emerge in the fourth century and beyond, the killing of the messiah took on new dimensions because now the Jews could be seen as god-killers (deicides). As the divinization of Jesus developed, the demonization of the Jews grew apace. Neither belief was a necessary development of New Testament ideas because of the diversity of elements in that book; they both evolved in the direction of the formulations of the post-Constantinian churches and sat easily with certain readings of the scriptures. Yet the demonization of the Jews is a fundamental element in the Fourth Gospel which fits neatly into the general focus of New Testament writings on the diabolical and the demonic. The extent to which the deity of Christ and the trinitarian nature of the divine are to be found at any point in the New Testament could be debated for ever, but the direct relationship between the Jews and the devil is explicit in it (note the metaphor 'synagogue of Satan' in Revelation 2.9; 3.9). Yet that explicit representation of the Jews need not have been developed outside certain writings of the early churches had there not been an ideological need to utilize it in the struggle for power and position over against Jewish communities in the late Roman period. By themselves the scriptures are relatively innocuous, but taken in conjunction with socio-economic situations and ideological needs certain hermeneutic choices can render even the innocuous positively dangerous. Confined to scripture, anti-Jewish rantings and polemics might have been harmless, but in the social context of communities vying for power and status Christians needed to develop powerful anti-Jewish propaganda in order to boost their own position. After Constantine power passed to the Christian churches – or to be precise, to some of them – and the Jewish communities were doomed in the long run. The development of the anti-Jewish polemics can be seen in a number of Christian writers (most notably St John Chrysostom), but the passion narratives and the Fourth Gospel had laid down the central foundations and terms of the debate and the polemics would only update the sentiments expressed by them.

Among the main charges made against the Jews in the patristic period, perhaps the most notable (from a modern viewpoint I think) was the sin of failing to recognize the messiah (Origen and Epiphanius). That is a charge straight out of the Gospels, especially the Fourth Gospel. It typifies a certain kind of Christian reaction to the Jews: how could anybody have failed to recognize the messiah? Such a failure must indicate a capacity for blindness or error almost beyond belief. A number of writers since included in the New Testament expressed their incredulity at such a possibility by citing Isaiah 6.9-10 (a difficult text in its original sense). And yet this 'blindness' has gone on now for almost a score of centuries. As neighbours of the Christian churches throughout Christian history the Jews have been a complete mystery. How could they both survive and fail to recognize Jesus as the messiah? It is an interesting question, with more than one answer to it. But, of course, we have only heard one side of the argument, in the New Testament and the continued repetition of that side throughout Christian history. Perhaps something should be said about the force of argument on the other side.

There is no argument from the other side! For Jewish reactions to Jesus and the rise of the Christian churches, we have only the writings contained in the New Testament. The other side is never represented. Later documents catch echoes of the debate, and certain developments in Jewish thinking may be explicable in terms of reactions to Christian readings of scripture. In the Talmud Jesus is regarded as a magician who led Israel astray, a Balaam. But we have nothing in Jewish sources which could reliably be dated to the first century. The extent to which the representation of the Jews in the Gospels and Acts is historically accurate is not a question we can answer from independent sources.

As propaganda, the New Testament cannot be regarded as a reliable source of historical information on the Jews. Occasionally an individual Jew or some Jews may be presented in positive terms (e.g. Nathanael in John 1.47; the Pharisee Nicodemus in John 3.1–15; the Pharisee Gamaliel in Acts 5.34–39), but the overwhelming tendency of the writings is to speak ill of the Jews. The savage attack on the scribes and the Pharisees in Matthew 23 hardly warrants the opinion that the Gospels provide an accurate and well-informed account of Jews or of their leaders. Only inasmuch as individual Jews or groups of Jews respond sympathetically to Jesus are Jews likely to be reported in a kindly fashion. As Jews cease to be good *torah*-respecting Jews and become Christians, they become acceptable in the New Testament writings. But as Jews faithful to the Mosaic law they are the target for abuse and merciless criticism: 'You serpents, you brood of vipers, how are you to escape being sentenced to Gehenna?' (Matt. 23.33).

It may be argued that the Jews of the New Testament belong to the symbolic forms of that book. That is, the term 'the Jews' is a cipher or a symbol of the opposition to Jesus and the Christians. Just as Herod represents a destructive, self-indulgent force in the New Testament, and Nazareth a place from which nothing good can come, so 'the Jews' is a mythic term to describe rivalry and opposition. As symbols such terms should not be confused with social realities bearing the same name. It is rather like Shakespeare's portrayals of Macbeth and Richard III – not to be confused with the historical personages of the same name. (The simile is not exact because there are connections between Shakespeare's characters and the historical figures behind them. Perhaps his Hamlet and the Danish king Amled would make a better comparison.) Provided the readers of the New Testament do not imagine that they are reading about the real, historical Jews when they encounter the term 'the Jews' in the Gospels and Acts, all may be well. It then becomes a question of how texts should be read. The scribes and Pharisees of Matthew 23 are creations of the writer, or symbols of attitudes which may be found among Christian leaders as much as among Jewish élites. The fact that outside the text there are such groups as Pharisees or Jews is neither here nor there and certainly should not be confused with the textual Pharisees or Jews. Much of the writing in the Gospels is highly conventional and uses citations, images and relations drawn from the Septuagint or other Greek versions of the Hebrew Bible. This mode of constructing narratives gives them such a textuality ('intertextuality' would be a better description) that it would be very unwise to assume the texts have any referentiality *outside* themselves and the world of the text created by the older scriptures and the writers of the Gospels. Hence 'the Jews' of the New Testament are a nasty bunch of vicious people who killed Jesus and persecuted the Christians. Like wicked stepmothers in fairy tales or ogres in folk tales, such Jews are the stock in trade of Gospel story writing, but not to be confused with real, living people.

The world of the text approach to reading the Bible is one of the best ways of reading such a literary production as the Bible. It resolves the insoluble problems of trying to relate the text to history, especially to the historical characters represented in the text. For example, the biblical Nebuchadrezzar is very different from what is known about the historical Babylonian emperor, just as the biblical Pontius Pilate is rather different from what little we know about the Roman procurator of Judaea who shared the same name. The historical personages have bequeathed their names to the text, but there the resemblances end. We know the technique from modern writing, where 'faction' combines fiction and fact by using real historical characters as figures in fiction writing (see the writings of E. L. Doctorow, Norman Mailer, D. M. Thomas).

However, whether we should apply such an analysis to ancient writings may be a more difficult question to answer. It works well, but until recently most readers of the Bible have pursued the more historical approach to reading such a text. While it must be apparent to any competent reader of the Gospels that the passion narratives are constructed from the Hebrew Bible, especially the lament psalms, religious readers of the New Testament have never allowed that obvious fact to interfere with their reading of them as straight historical reportage. But if the story of the betrayal, seizure, trial and execution of Jesus is a construction from various sources as well as being a dramatic narration of a timeless scene of betrayal and death, what connection need it have with any historical circumstances?

Every character in the story plays a preordained role, scripted in the past (cf. Matt. 26.56) without the power of autonomous action (cf. John 19.10–11). These formal and symbolic structures of the story need have little or nothing to do with historical events. That does not mean there never was a crucifixion of Jesus. It does mean that the representation of such an event by the passion narratives of the Gospels is something other than the reporting of that fact. According to Paul, the facts received by him and passed on to others were 'Christ died . . . was buried . . . was raised . . .' (1 Cor. 15.1–4). Such facts leave ample room for developing into a sustained narrative of plot and counterplot, conspiracy and denial, power plays and cowardice.

Modern readings of ancient texts cannot escape history quite as easily as the preceding two paragraphs suggest. What I have written may well be a correct statement of the way the passion narratives were constructed – there is no way of finding out – but it is not how the Gospels have been read from time immemorial. The Jews in the story may be ciphers created by Christian communities as the necessary foil to their claims about Jesus. However, the common term shared by 'the Jews' of the Gospels and the real members of the Jewish people – namely the description 'Jew' – has throughout history been sufficient identification for the vast majority of Christian readers of the Gospels. For them there has been a clear common identity between Jews and 'the Jews', and they have held *all* Jews responsible for the murder of Christ. No amount of sophisticated modern readings of texts will persuade them otherwise. Not even the rise of critical theology has changed that attitude to reading the Gospels.

The problem of history for New Testament texts

Two points are being made here. The question of reading – a subtext of this whole book – and the problem of history for texts. Nothing can now remove from the canon of Christian scriptures the vilification of the Jews, nor can history be rewritten in order to write out of it the Christian treatment of Jews. What are the connections between this history and these scriptures? I have already said that there is not a simple one-to-one correspondence between text and belief. Good Christian folk did not hear the Gospels read to them and then rush out into the streets in order to butcher Jews. There were, I grant you, occasions when Christians heard the Easter sermons of their bishops and did rush out to murder Jews. But the connections were generally more complex and determined by prevailing socio-economic and ideological factors. Even so, I am arguing in this chapter that the real mischief lies in the scriptures and in that portrayal of the people of the Jews. Little or nothing in the New Testament ever militated against Christian antisemitism. If the foundation documents of the Gospels identify the Jews as the enemies of Jesus, Paul and the churches, then wherever and whenever Christians come into contact with Jews, antagonistic responses are bound to follow. The whole history of Christian antisemitism testifies to that diagnosis. The problem of history for the New Testament is well focused by the history of antisemitism. While the structures and substance of antisemitic laws imposed by the churches on the Jews belong to the post-biblical period, and over many centuries created the image of the Jew which did much to fuel the rise of modern European antisemitism, that history of anti-Jewish beliefs and practices found its justification and rationale in the New Testament. *There* is the problem of the Christian Bible for the modern reader. It is impossible to read the representation of the Jews in the Gospels and Acts today without feeling the horror surface in oneself because one knows the end of that story. From the depiction of the people of the Jews as opponents, persecutors and murderers of Jesus and many early Christians in New Testament times, through the representations of the Jews as devil-worshippers and killers of Christian children in late medieval times, to the black propaganda of Julius Streicher and Joseph Goebbels in the Third Reich, there is a long unholy history of consistent crusading against the Jews. I am *not* saying that the New Testament is responsible for the Nazi genocide programme against the Jews. I am saying that moral responsibility for contributing to the long history of antisemitic cruelty can be laid at the doors of some of the New Testament writers. It may not have been their intention – who can say what they had in mind with their hostile presentation of the Jews? – but time and Christian ideology would be able to build on their foundation and, in the fullness of time, the number of murdered Jews would belittle the crucifixion itself. But how responsible are people for what others do with their words?

If the relation between texts and history is highly problematic, the question of how texts should be read is equally problem-laden.

Trying to make sense of what the early Christian writers had to say about the Jews forces the reader to develop a reading strategy in order to take seriously what they wrote. No doubt there was opposition from Jewish communities to the emergent Christian groups, and the developing hermeneutic and practical differences between them inevitably made for antagonistic relations. After centuries of conflict over shared interests (the element of conflict should not be overemphasized as there is evidence of friendly relations between churches and synagogues at certain times in parts of the empire) it is hardly surprising that when orthodox churches began to assume imperial power the Jews should begin to suffer. That is the pattern of political struggle which we know all too well from the twentieth century with its gulags and death camps. The *Realpolitik* of Christian imperialism explains the formalization of rules against the Jews, while the earlier conflict between Jews and Christians over messianic and other interpretations of scripture reflects their competing claims for living space in the Roman empire. Part of any such struggle is inevitably the abuse of opponents, and in inheriting the Bible the Christian communities acquired a book much devoted to the abuse of opposition. A reading of the Hebrew Bible in conjunction with the Talmuds will reveal a world of rhetorical abuse unlike anything else in world literature. Christian writers learned well from their reading of the Bible, and the patristic writers developed an equally virulent invective in their polemical writings (e.g. Jerome, Tertullian).

One strategy of reading the Gospels would be to treat them as Jewish writings like the prophetic books in the Hebrew Bible. In the prophets one of the dominant modes of discourse is rhetorical abuse of the community. Very strong language, often obscene (read Ezekiel chapters 16, 20, 23), is used against cities and communities. Invective, rage, irony and satire are striking features of these books. People are never accused of making mistakes or of failing to live up to an ideal, they are accused of adultery and murder, of worshipping false gods and lying, of cannibalism and robbery (e.g. Mic. 3.1–3; Isa. 59.1–8; 65.1–7; Ezek. 22.23–31). The history of Jerusalem is presented as one long story of rebellion against Yahweh (e.g. Jer. 32.28–35; cf. the letter to Artaxerxes written by Rehum and his companions in Ezra 4.7–16). This type of rhetorical overkill is such a feature of biblical writing that it is difficult not to read Matthew 23 as one more instance of it. The 'woe oracle' of the prophets (e.g. Isa. 5.8–23; Hab. 2.6–19) is replicated by the writer in a magnificent chain of 'Woe to you, scribes and Pharisees' pieces which culminates in a lament over Jerusalem the killer of prophets (Matt. 23.37). We do not possess any historical information which would render any of these harangues other than rhetorical. The rant factor being so dominant in prophecy, it would be a pity to render the rhetoric prosaic by matching it to a social reality. The reading strategy developed here does not involve seeing the prophetic invective as a description of the social world of the speaker, but reads it as a rhetorical style decontextualized from having any referent outside of the text. Hence the scribes and Pharisees of Matthew 23 are not to be confused with real flesh and blood Jews but are to be seen as characters in a world constructed by the text.

The textual world of the Gospels represents the people of the Jews as conspirators and wicked people, just as the prophets had depicted the people of Israel as vicious and beyond redemption. The long history of killing the prophets by the Jewish people comes to an end with the killing of Jesus. Paul makes a similar charge to the one made by Matthew 23.37 when he writes to the church of the Thessalonians in the following stereotypical fashion:

> For you, brethren, became imitators of the churches of God in Christ Jesus which are in Judea; for you suffered the same things from your own countrymen as they did from *the Jews, who killed both the Lord Jesus and the prophets,* and drove us out, and displease God and oppose all men by hindering us from speaking to the Gentiles that they may be saved – *so as always to fill up the measure of their sins.* But God's wrath has come upon them at last. (1 Thess. 2.14–16)

The final phrase of that statment is ambiguous: the Greek words *eis telos* can mean 'to the end' in the sense of 'until the end', or 'at last' in the sense of 'finally', or 'for ever' in the sense of 'through all eternity' (a frequent use in the Septuagint), or 'fully' in the sense of 'decisively'. Paul may be saying that finally the divine anger has caught up with the Jews or he may be expressing the opinion that God's anger has come upon the Jews permanently. The killing of Jesus did the trick and divine outrage is now completely unleashed against them. Whatever the nuance of expression – and ambiguity is a constant in biblical writings – Paul incorporates his own experience of Jewish opposition into the history of killing the prophets and makes this history the grounds for divine wrath against the Jews.

The Jews and Jesus as Messiah

Paul's view that God's anger has now come upon the Jews suggests a different opinion from that expressed in Romans 9—11, for it hints at a permanent wrath against them. Perhaps it is only a note of exasperation (catching the tone in a piece of writing is a very difficult thing to do and is one of the areas where speech is superior to writing) because the Jews not only refuse to believe in Jesus but also hinder others from doing so. Impatience and exasperation with the Jewish refusal to believe in Jesus will become a common theme in Christian writings over the centuries. Much of Martin Luther's outrageous invective against the Jews stems from an all-too-Christian incapacity to appreciate the position of the Jews on the subject of Jesus as messiah. Jews are only to be tolerated as potential converts to Christianity. If they convert then they demonstrate the truth of Christian claims. But if they do not convert they pose a problem. The conventional and biblical explanation for such a refusal would be the deuteronomistic charge, 'You are a stiff-necked people' (Deut. 9.6, 13). However, Jews could hardly deny Moses and convert to Christianity without offending against the deuteronomistic law itself. There is perhaps an element of irony here in that the very language of *torah* could be used against the Jews themselves. Fidelity to that revelation entailed rejection of the Christian proclamation of Jesus as messiah.

To the modern reader of the Gospels, especially one trained in the critical reading of texts, the claim that the Jews *failed* to recognize Jesus *as messiah* is an absurd one. Assuming an atmosphere of messianic expectations in first-century Judaea - an assumption without much support outside carefully selected texts - we would have to define the substance of such expectations in terms of Hebrew Bible, specific communities (e.g. Qumran) and special writings (e.g. apocalypses). In essence messiah - again making the assumption that only *one* messiah was expected - would be a great warrior of Davidic proportions who would free the Jewish people from the yoke of foreign domination (i.e. Rome), restore power to the temple-city of Jerusalem, and make the nations subservient to Israel. Great wealth would flow into Jerusalem and the nations would make pilgrimages there in order to learn the divine *torah*. Peace and justice would reign supreme throughout the land – and the world.

Nothing in this job specification fits the Jesus of the Gospels. The wandering charismatic prophet from Galilee known as 'Jesus of Nazareth' has no connections with any messianic expectation set out in the messianic reading of the Hebrew Bible. There are plain attempts by the Gospel writers to link the birth and life of Jesus with biblical texts interpreted messianically. Few of them work at all, and they are so clearly impositions on the narrative that they only reflect the convictions of the writers about Jesus *as* the messiah. For example, in spite of Matthew's use of Isaiah 7.14 we have no evidence that Jesus was ever known as 'Immanuel of Bethlehem' (Matt. 1.23–25). Matthew's use of scripture in chapters 1—4 is too wide-ranging and allusive to count as evidence for anything other than the complex 'textuality' – the world created by the text – of the Gospel writer.

The claim that Jesus of Nazareth was the messiah is a special pleading type of claim. Early Christian communities preached about the death and resurrection of Jesus (cf. Acts 2—4) and by dint of certain types of exegesis made connections between the death of Jesus and metaphors in the psalms and the prophets. New interpretations of old texts were required to fit Jesus into a messianic scheme of expectation. The letter to the Hebrews is a very good example of how much the Hebrew Bible had to be reinterpreted to be accommodated to the Christian proclamation of Jesus as messiah. Only by rewriting the texts could the claim be sustained at any level.

Such rewriting is always the function of the hermeneutic of reading. Reading old texts in the light of the events surrounding the life and death of Jesus gave to those texts *new* significance. But the texts relating to messianic expectations were seldom used, because the Jesus figure failed to fulfil any and every specification of that ancient hope. The Jewish people did not find themselves in charge of their own land, nor did they experience the sweeping away of the Roman imperial power. Peace and justice did not become the dominant features of Palestinian life after the death of Jesus. Now it may be said that of course none of these things happened because some Jews rejected Jesus, or the Jews *as a people* failed to recognize him as the messiah. These are Christian rationalizations. The texts which are used to construct the substance of the belief in a messiah know nothing of a messianic failure. They are not formulated in that fashion. Furthermore, Jesus is not represented in the Gospels as going about preaching himself *as the messiah*, so any rejection of his message could not be understood as a concomitant refusal to recognize him as messiah. Mark's Gospel uses the notion of a messianic *secret* to organize much of its presentation of Jesus – secrecy is fundamentally important in that Gospel (e.g. 3.12; 5.43; 7.36; 8.30; 9.9). The confession that Jesus *is* the messiah made by Peter is also subject to secrecy (Matt. 16.20; Mark 8.30; Luke 9.21). So how could the Jews have known that Jesus was the messiah in the first place?

Clearly the Gospel writers had a major problem with the reception of Jesus by the Jews. If Jesus really had been the messiah, then the Jews would have flocked to him – at least those Jews who believed in such a being as the messiah (contrary to popular belief such a belief was not a necessary part of Jewish religion). As Christians the Gospel writers believed Jesus to be the messiah, but also knew that the Jewish people had not believed him to be such. Different explanations are provided in the Gospels to account for this problem. (A problem not unlike that surrounding beliefs about the Grand Duchess Anastasia – some people believe she survived the Bolshevik massacre of the Czar's family in 1918, others believe she did not.) Resolving the problem is extremely difficult. One outstanding problem facing the Gospel writers is that of explaining how Jesus could be both the messiah of Israel *and* also be rejected by the Jewish people. If the Jewish family did not recognize their own messiah – then what price messiah? The notion that Jesus was not the messiah does not appear to have been entertained at all by the New Testament writers. While much of the writing is devoted to proclaiming Jesus as the son of God, the identification of him as the messiah is so entrenched that it becomes incorporated into the name by which he is now best known – Jesus *Christ*.

Among the explanations used by the Gospel writers to account for the Jewish rejection of Jesus as the messiah the most popular one is derived from Isaiah 6.9–10 (Septuagint version, with variations). Most of the Gospels cite it (e.g. Matt. 13.14–15; Mark 8.18; John 12.40; cf. Luke 8.10; Acts 28.26–27). The variations in the use of the Isaiah material in the different Gospels cannot disguise the important part it plays in providing the writers with a possible explanation for the reception of Jesus by the Jews. Those who accepted him were those who could *see* the truth about him, whereas these who rejected him were blind. This blindness having been self-induced –

only Mark 4.12 retains any sense of the Hebrew original which makes the action of the speaker the cause of the blindness – the Jews reject the messiah out of the hardness of their own hearts. So the problem of the Jewish rejection of Jesus is resolved to the satisfaction of the Gospel writers. Isaiah 6.9–10 is a very tricky and difficult text, so it is hardly surprising that it should complicate the Gospel material as well. As an explanation of the reason for teaching by parables it sits ill with other passages in the Gospels which represent Jesus as being heard gladly by the crowds. What it does achieve for the parables is to convert them into teaching for the élite. The crowds can appreciate the miracles (e.g. Matt. 15.29–31), but the teaching is strictly for the élitist disciples. Once this kind of argument is introduced into any debate, problems can be solved to the satisfaction of one side. Blindness and insight allow the same event to function in differentiating ways.

The use of Isaiah 6.9–10 to account for the Jewish rejection of Jesus and the preaching of the gospel continues the critique of the prophets by other means. It picks up elements of stubbornness and blindness among the people (as well as isolating an élite of privileged hearers) and makes these the cause of the refusal to hear the messiah to the point of believing in him. It is a nice example of the interpretation of scripture being used against the community to whom the scriptures belonged. But the extent to which it is a successful defence of the Christian belief about Jesus as messiah is impossible to determine without having access to the Jewish side of the argument. Many centuries later, when Rabbi Moses ben Nachman (Ramban) debated the matter with Fra Paulo Christiani in public before King Jayme I of Aragon (in 1263), he made the point:

> . . . since in your opinion Jesus was divine, he was better equipped with knowledge and ability to establish his own claims than is the king, and *if our fathers who saw him and were acquainted with him did not listen to him*, how then shall we believe and listen to the king who has no knowledge of him in actual experience but only through a remote report which he has heard from men who did not know Jesus and were not Jesus' countrymen as were our fathers who knew him and were witnesses . . . ? (*emphases added*)

It is a very good point. It also makes a point opposite to that made by the Gospel writers. It should warn the modern reader of the New Testament that there is another side to the argument. Also it should remind that reader about the propagandist nature of the Gospel writings. The Gospels make no secret about being propaganda. They are designed to persuade the reader/hearer of the truth of what they have to say (e.g. Luke 1.4; John 20.31), but they are not philosophical discourses setting out arguments for and against specific positions. The other side is never heard.

The survival of the Jews after the Roman destruction of Jerusalem c.70 CE and the emergence of rabbinic Judaism as the precursor of what later became known as orthodox Judaism, meant that the Christian churches did not replace Judaism so much as create parallel and alternative religious communities. Jews went on living in Jewish communities and developing a ritual world with its own scriptures and important writings. Their fate in the Christian imperium was a harsh one but they survived all over Europe until the Nazi regime turned a long history of Christian antisemitism into a technologized nightmare of extermination. The Nuremberg laws enacted many of the rulings against the Jews first developed by Christian councils. In the disappearance of European Jewry intended by the 'final solution' of the Third Reich may be glimpsed the final stages of Paul's notion of the divine wrath permanently come upon the Jews. This side of Auschwitz, it may be salutary to read again the New Testament and the long history of Christian antisemitism and to appreciate the problem constituted by the New Testament in the light thrown by the ovens of the Third Reich. Throughout Christian history the Jews have been the bad conscience of the churches. They have been the neighbour who was outside the commandment to love the neighbour. This outsider role can only be accounted for on the grounds of the representation of the Jews in the New Testament and the subsequent rivalry of Jews and Christians for political space in the Roman empire.

There is an explanation which belongs to Christian apologetics. It would explain the plight of the Jews as being directly related to their rejection of the messiah. It is an argument rather similar to the deuteronomistic representation of the fall of Jerusalem in 587 BCE in terms of abandoning the covenant:

And many nations will pass by this city, and every man will say to his neighbour, 'Why has Yahweh dealt thus with this great city?' And they will answer, 'Because they forsook the covenant of Yahweh their God, and worshipped other gods and served them.' (Jer. 22.8-9)

The Jews rejected messiah and had him murdered, so they have suffered appallingly ever since for their sins. It is a glib explanation which carries very little weight. In contradistinction to the dramatized explanation I have cited from the book of Jeremiah, it may be said of the Jews that they did *not* abandon the worship of God. On the contrary, they clung to that worship and out of loyalty to the *torah* they refused to go after other gods. It would be an irony of cosmic proportions if that fidelity should have been rewarded with a history of suffering because they were wrong to remain faithful to *torah*! In a sense it is the reverse of the charge in Jeremiah. The Christian explanation is naïve. It is naïve because the sufferings of the Jews over nearly twenty centuries have been inflicted on them by the Christians – not by God. The commandments to do good and to love others have been violated by Christian communities in their treatment of the Jews. Unless the wrath of Christians is the equivalent of the wrath of God there is no need to look for explanations beyond the behaviour of Christians towards Jews to explain Christian antisemitism.

A Jewish response to such awful suffering perpetuated over so many centuries might take many forms, but the usual explanation in theological terms is adequate. If Jews faithfully serve God then they will inevitably suffer because they live among the wicked and the godless. In the words of the lament, 'For your sake we are slain all the day long, and accounted as sheep for the slaughter' (Psalm 44.22). Such suffering is a sign of fidelity to the covenant – this is a reversal of the deuteronomistic type of argument used in the Hebrew Bible where suffering is a sign of the broken covenant. It did not take the ancient Jews very long to work out the inadequacies of the deuteronomistic viewpoint. The book of Job, the lament psalms, Qoheleth, the books of the Maccabees, and centuries of experience of the imperial rule of Babylon, Persia, Greece, Rome and Christendom all underwrote what they knew only too well. Those in power dominate the powerless and the tender mercies of the wicked are cruel. There is also the point made by Herman Melville: 'Hapless are the favorites of heaven'. To be God's chosen people is to be in trouble all day long. It goes with the territory. It is an explanation of sorts. If the world is genuinely godless and if the ungodly are in power, then religious communities will find life rather difficult for themselves. Such alternative explanations will function better than claims about being under a divine curse for rejecting the messiah nearly two thousand years ago. They will also contribute something to explaining the awful suffering caused by the Third Reich. The wholesale extermination of Jewish communities by the Nazi regime cannot be attributed to the so-called curse caused by rejecting messiah. The Jews of Europe were no more guilty of having rejected Jesus than the Jews of America (the whole notion of a curse is silly beyond words, but it belongs to Christian propaganda against the Jews so I use it here) yet only they suffered the onslaught of the Nazi war machine. For the very orthodox Jews the Hitler massacres were not essentially different from Christian crusades and pogroms, they were just more intensive forms of persecution for being Jewish. They represented the suffering which is the concomitant of being faithful to the covenant. What can you expect from the *goyim*? Hitler was just the latest form or incarnation of that old enemy, the Amalekite Haman (see the book of Esther).

The death camps of the Hitler war raise too many painful issues for an adequate discussion here. Auschwitz casts a long, dark shadow over the doing of theology, especially in a Christian context. The problem of evil bears on the matter and that is too big a subject to slip into the closing pages of this chapter. However Jews may handle the many problems raised by the extermination camps, there are major issues facing Christian theology too. After Auschwitz it becomes harder to go on doing traditional Christian theology because what happened to the Jews there reflects badly on Christian attitudes to Jews as well as posing questions for theology. Some recognition of these factors has occurred since the war, but the question about the problematic of the New Testament remains. In the light of Auschwitz – and should theology be done in any other light now? – the New Testament depictions of the Jews become more than just rhetoric. We must ask about the connections between such rhetoric and what has happened to real Jews throughout the centuries of Christendom's domination of European civilization. Given the events of the twentieth century, the representation of the Jews in John and Acts takes on a different and more chilling aspect.

The New Testament cannot be rewritten. What is written in it is written (cf. John 19.21–22). But interpretation and reading are always ways of rewriting. The reinterpreted text is a rewritten one. So after the rituals of repentance for what has been done to the Jews over the centuries, new readings of the text will control the anti-Jewish elements in it. They will be recognized as conventional genres of abusing the community in terms of the ranting prophet's diatribes. What is going on in the Gospels – the subtext of the anti-Jewish material – is an example of the standard demonization of the enemy so characteristic of political propaganda. Parallels can be seen in the Hebrew Bible. In that collection of books the Canaanites are demonized and assigned to extermination by holy war and ideological campaigns (e.g. Deut. 20.16–18; the book of Joshua). Whether such wars of annihilation were ever practised in reality or simply belong to the ideological writings of the deuteronomistic school is unimportant for my purposes here (and besides there is no way of determining the matter now). So much of the religion of the Hebrew Bible belongs to Canaanite belief and practice that we must understand the strictures against the banned nations as a way of distancing the 'new' religion from its all too obvious roots. By denying and opposing the antecedents of the community, justifications could be found for development.

Similar moves can be seen in the New Testament. Taking over some of the beliefs and practices of the Jewish communities of their time, the Christian churches also wished to distance themselves from being Jewish. The Pauline charge of 'judaizing' – a charge much heard again in Reformation times – indicates the conscious desire to overcome the past. Hence the opponents of Jesus are always the Jews, especially the Pharisees, scribes, priests and Sadducees. The amount of anti-Jewish invective in the Gospels is only explicable in terms of profound rivalry felt by the Christian writers for the Jewish communities which occupied the same social space as did the Christian churches. Surely the Gospels could have been written without so much anti-Jewish polemic? The Synoptic Gospels may show much less of it than the Fourth Gospel, but even they indulge in it from time to time. What the Jews did to the Canaanites in the Hebrew Bible, the Christians did to the Jews in the New Testament! The denial of legitimacy to the other, the denigration of the other in extreme terms, and the takeover of the other's religion (at a reinterpreted level of course) are part of the dynamics of political struggle. What makes things so much more complicated in the Bible is the fact that the developing Christian communities took over the Hebrew scriptures as well, so that the text and its reinterpretations exist side by side. This complicates things very much because it leaves the older text available for and vulnerable to changing patterns of reading. That is why the critical reading of scripture had such a devastating effect on traditional modes of interpreting the Bible. The oddity is the Christian Bible consisting of Old Testament (Hebrew Bible in Greek/Latin) and New Testament. In Jewish circles the scriptures remained the Hebrew Bible, but the ways of reading that collection were embodied in many writings (especially the Talmuds but not the Mishnah) which were not themselves scripture. The Christian reinterpretation of Jewish scripture was appended to those scriptures, and unequally yoked together they have been problematic ever since.

A hermeneutic of reading may be able to control whatever the text says. Hence the anti-Jewish material in the New Testament may be susceptible to nuanced readings which will defuse the danger it constitutes for Jewish-Christian relations. A critical reading of the Bible can certainly handle the material without difficulty and render it safe for modern consumption. I do not mean by that comment that the critical approach to the Bible should domesticate the book. I mean that the offensive material on the Jews can be understood in context and not turned into statements about real Jews in the world outside the text. Otherwise the New Testament remains unharnessed by a reading ethic and the roots of Christian antisemitism will flourish again. Already antisemitism is re-emerging all over Europe, especially in eastern European countries where once the iron fist of communism kept certain forms of nationalistic antisemitism in check.

Texts can be dangerous, even deadly. So reading strategies are required to act as flak jackets. Wrong or inappropriate readings of books can be equally dangerous. In the era of Salman Rushdie and the appalling controversy over his magical realism novel *The Satanic Verses* it requires no argument from me to make the point about the importance of knowing *how to read* books. The misreading of *The Satanic Verses* as a historical critique of Islam and its holy prophet rather than as a postmodernist, magical realism novel has already caused a number of deaths and made for untold trouble between different cultures. Rushdie's novel provides a rather good parallel to reading the New Testament on the subject of the Jews. If we take the New Testament at face value – one of the worst ways of reading is the 'face value' approach – then it is easy to imagine the subsequent history of Christian antisemitism. But should we read the Gospels, Acts and Paul in such a way that we confuse textual Jews with real Jews? The wrong reading of a book can be fatal.

A different example of how dangerous a wrong reading or

misreading of a book can be is afforded by Mark Chapman's reading of J. D. Salinger's immortal *The Catcher in the Rye*. Who, of a certain age, has not read that novel and not imagined themselves as Holden Caulfield? In that sense Mark Chapman was just a normal reader of the novel who imagined himself as Holden Caulfield and set out to clean up the phonies in the world. But his reading of it, among many other things no doubt, sent him out to shoot the Beatle John Lennon. On 8 December 1980 Chapman, having lived as Holden Caulfield for years in his head, shot and killed John Lennon. Some reading of *The Catcher in the Rye*! Books can kill – no, *readers* of books do the killing; books can inspire people to kill other people. It's all very well to say, the letter kills, the spirit gives life (2 Cor. 3.6) – it was the spirit of *Catcher* as understood by Mark Chapman which contributed to Lennon's death as much as some of the letters in that book. But it is a strange reading of *Catcher* that it should send out one reader to murder. History is full of such misreadings. The Bible shares in much of that history of misreading. The people of the Jews have suffered greatly from readings of the New Testament, but whether those readings were misreadings is part of the problem constituted by the New Testament.

It will be obvious to some readers of this chapter that I have not given much attention to the possibility that the Gospel writers and Paul were simply describing their experiences of Jews and so were writing historically accurate depictions of Jews. I do not think that viewpoint can be sustained by argument, so I have not devoted much space to it. I have, however, emphasized by my chapter title that the problem concerns 'the people of the Jews' and not individual Jews or groups of them. The New Testament identifies the Jewish people as the problem and berates it for murdering Christ. The writers of the Fourth Gospel and Acts regularly identify 'the Jews' as the trouble-makers rather than small groups of Jews. It is not possible to regard the passion narratives as reportage. Consummate drama they may be, patchwork quilts of quotation and symbol manipulation they may also be, but descriptions of what actually happened when Christ was slain seems the least likely explanation. The rhetoric of the stories is too conventional and contrived and the characters too stereotypical and unreal (e.g. vicious Jews, benign Romans!) for realism here to have historical referents. And it is because the narratives are so rhetorical in their constructions, that how they are read becomes so important for their interpretation. The problem of antisemitism may not yield to techniques of reading – it is too late for that in the light of what has happened in history – but it may be possible to redeem the New Testament from evil for generations to come by developing more sophisticated strategies of reading it. Otherwise it will be as the poet said: 'Odour of blood when Christ was slain/Made all Platonic tolerance vain.'

5
Wolf in Sheep's Clothing

I think we ought to read only the kind of books that wound and stab us . . . We need the books that affect us like a disaster, that grieve us deeply, like the death of someone we loved more than ourselves, like being banished into forests far from everyone, like a suicide. A book must be the axe for the frozen sea inside us.

Franz Kafka

for there's no place therein
that does not see you. You must change your life.

Rainer Maria Rilke

The problematics of reading the Bible, in whatever version, and the problematics of that collection of books for theology and the modern age, are readily recognized by everybody familiar with Bible and theology. The various examples which I have discussed in the previous four chapters are merely a scratching of the surface. Many more chapters could be written on the subject and a far greater range of paradigmatic issues could have been discussed. Any use of a series of books produced in the Iron Age and complemented by writings from the time of imperial Rome is bound to have problems of understanding, and more especially of application. If such a collection of writings, in whatever form or language, is also incorporated into church structures and bound up in the service of (alien) philosophical-theological systems of thought, then the problematics of the book will be increased at a rate beyond human resolution. Some of the problems can be dealt with by embracing the modern critical approach to the Bible, with its historical-critical reading of texts and its engagement with contemporary scientific worldviews. Critical theology can find a perspective for reading the Bible without having to imagine that it is either problem-free or not deformed by its encounter with the Procrustean nature of ecclesiastical control. There are gains and losses in this approach, and the critical reading of the Bible cannot conceal the real problems which remain however the Bible is read.

Each chapter in this book might have had a very different content if I had focused on other aspects of the problem. The topics chosen represent only a few possible approaches to understanding the nature of the Bible as a fundamental problem for interpretation in the contemporary world. Of course the problem is not new. Every serious reader of the Bible, in whatever version or language, since a codex of the Bible (Latin/Greek) first came into existence, has had profound problems dealing with it. A careful reading of Augustine's *Confessions* (especially books XI—XIII where he is trying to explain Genesis 1) will reveal the struggles of a reader for whom the text is (literally) the word of God. Augustine needed to splice biblical thought with philosophical ideas in order to create his theology, so he faced specific problems which he resolved, to some extent, to his own satisfaction. Without philosophy Augustine would not have been the man he became, and his reading of the Bible owed much to his philosophical conversion as well as to his becoming a Christian. But everybody reads in a similar fashion, for without the reader's own experiences, outlook and beliefs, texts remain silent. How the individual reader deals with a specific text depends on what the reader brings to the text; and texts then mean – are made to mean – a hybrid formed of what is written and what the reader already knows. Of course the process is often much more dynamic than this bald statement of it. The problematics of a text can force the reader to work hard at *extracting* sense from what is written (the appropriate verb will vary from reader to reader) in the company of whatever guides may be available, and assisted by *how* the individual reader reads. Augustine is just one example among thousands of readers of the Bible who might have been adduced to make the same point.

The modern reader is startled by the sheer range of the problem of reading and applying the Bible today. How can a book in which slavery and xenophobia are advocated at such a level of intensity be of any relevance to contemporary thought? In the modern world of participatory democracies, talk about kings and kingdoms, slaves and servants, is hardly likely to appeal much to intelligent readers. Rules designed to control pastoralist and agricultural communities are bound to be inadequate to post-industrial societies. Contemporary ideologies and critiques of consumerist cultures – such as feminism or communism – will find the Bible virtually unreadable because its values will appear antiquarian and obsolete. Where concubines and slave-girls are an integral part of the biblical social world, and witches and sorcerers ply their trade, it is difficult to imagine a direct connection between the Bible and contemporary life. Outside of European culture (and its offshoot the United States) some of these features of the world of the Bible may well find echoes in the social structures of other cultures. Biblical genealogies and tribal kin systems might find a ready appreciation in Africa, and the world of magic behind so much of the Bible would have links with various cultures in other parts of the world. But for Western people a great deal of the Bible is, at best, a book of ancient history with some interesting elements of social anthropology included in it.

All these observations are a fair representation of how the Bible is perceived by many (non) readers of it in modern life. The ecclesiastical concerns with the different editions of the Bible give it an institutional role which need not concern anybody outside the churches (or synagogues, *mutatis mutandis*). In the academy and other cultural circles the Bible – especially as a book in translation – is a work of literature and may be read and studied as such. Its status as sacred scripture need be of little or no concern to the *literati* who handle it as a cultural object; at least of no more concern than the fact that Homer once functioned as sacred text for the ancient Greeks. For religious people the Bible will have a wide range of functions and will be viewed in many different ways. It may be treated as an inspired (and inspiring) collection of authoritative writings of a canonic nature (i.e. normative), and interpreted in accordance with the rules and practices of specific traditions. On the other hand, it may be regarded as a charm, a commodity or a fetish. That is, in religious circles its status as a bestseller (commodity) may be important and it may make an ideal christening present (rigged out in a special edition). For some it will have the function of a magical charm and will be carried around on important occasions. For others it will be treated like a lottery or a bran tub and dipped into at random in order to provide guidance for daily living (fetish). It would take another book to discuss all the different uses to which the Bible has been put over the many centuries of its existence. I mention a few here just to indicate the different levels at which it may be read and to note some of the ways it functions in contemporary society. My main interest in this chapter, however, is with the Bible as a serious religious/literary work which has had profound significance for so many of its readers over the centuries since it emerged *as a book*. This importance of the book cannot be gainsaid, and I wish only to focus on some aspects of the problem of taking it seriously as something which does or should affect one's life.

All silliness apart (by 'silly' I mean such trivialized uses of the Bible as a fetish typified by all those pocket New Testaments with bullet holes in them which were popular after the Great War as testimonies to the prophylactic qualities of the 'good book'), the claim that the Bible has been very important for individuals and communities requires no documentation. St Thomas Aquinas thought of himself as *homo unius libri*, 'a man of one book', and that book was the Bible. Since Gutenberg introduced printing into Europe and the Reformation made Bibles important for ordinary literate people, the book, in various editions and forms, has been the lifeblood of many pious people, educated or otherwise. John Bunyan described his conversion as having come after he had been 'killed by the authority of the holy Scriptures' and, no doubt, many thousands of Christians since then would testify to similar experiences and would ascribe many important features of their lives to the influence of that book. Its significance for religious people – not to mention thoughtful but non-religious persons – cannot be over-exaggerated. An inscription in a Bible found at Majdanek (one of the Nazi slave and extermination camps) says it all:

> Good brother in freedom
> This is all that I own.
> Take this Bible, carry it further
> Into eternity – if you can.

Augustine, in one of the most famous passages in his *Confessions* (book VIII chapter 12), tells the story of how on one occasion he was so depressed and in despair over the grip his lower nature had on him that he left his companion Alypius and flung himself under a fig tree in order to burst into tears. Weeping and asking questions – Augustine was an inveterate asker of questions (*quare . . . quare . . . quare*, why? . . . why? . . . why?) – he suddenly heard the sing-song voice of a child repeating the refrain *tolle, lege*, 'take, read, take, read.' He understood these words to be a divine command instructing him to open his book of scripture and to read the first passage his eyes should fall on. Reflecting on Antony's experience of responding to the reading of the Gospel heard when he had happened to go into a church, Augustine writes:

> So I hurried back to the place where Alypius was sitting, for when I stood up to move away I had put down the book containing Paul's Epistles. I seized it and opened it, *and in silence I read* the first passage on which my eyes fell: *Not in revelling and drunkenness, not in lust and wantonness, not in quarrels and rivalries. Rather, arm yourself with the Lord Jesus Christ; spend no more thought on nature and nature's appetites.* I had no wish to read more and no need to do so. For in an instant, as I came to the end of the sentence, it was as though the light of confidence flooded into my heart and all the darkness of doubt was dispelled.   (*emphases added*)

The fortuitous – Augustine would not have so described it! – encounter with a text directly relevant to his situation, converted Augustine from all thought of marriage and reproduction and also overjoyed his mother by confirming an old dream of hers. Augustine's reading of Romans 13.13–14 also assisted his companion Alypius who, on being informed by Augustine of what had happened, read the text and continued his reading beyond Augustine's portion to find in 14.1 a statement which he could apply to himself. (In citing this well-known section from the *Confessions* I have emphasized the phrase 'and in silence I read', because it indicates an important shift in the social habit of reading from that of reading aloud (remember the Ethiopian official in Acts 8) to that of reading silently (eye over mouth). Other fascinating features of the section I shall leave for the reader to discover.)

Another account of an encounter with the Bible which changed a life, almost as famous (among English-speaking people) as Augustine's, is that described by the English Puritan writer John Bunyan. His great work *The Pilgrim's Progress* (1678; the original title is much longer than the three words by which it is known) is an allegorical tale told as a dream and its first sentences are among the great opening lines of world literature:

> As I walked through the wilderness of this world, I lighted on a certain place, where was a den; and I laid me down in that place to

sleep: and as I slept I dreamed a dream. I dreamed, and behold I saw a man clothed with rags, standing in a certain place, with his face from his own house, *a book in his hand*, and a great burden upon his back. I looked, *and saw him open the book, and read therein; and as he read, he wept and trembled*: and not being able to contain, he brake out with a lamentable cry; saying, 'What shall I do?' (*emphases added*)

The book, of course, is the Bible and the figure, whose name is Christian, was in the habit of reading it and becoming greatly distressed. His reading of the Bible had convinced him of his lost and doomed state; a state and a reading which evoked from him the famous cry 'What shall I do to be saved?' (cf. Acts 16.30). The burden on his back had come about by reading the book and, after many temporizing encounters with other people and much instruction from godly persons, he was enabled to lose it when he arrived at a place where there stood a Cross.

These two stories are among the best known accounts of the role of the Bible in transforming the reader's life. While it would be unwise to take them at face value because they were written a considerable time after the events and, like the passion narratives in the Gospels, reveal the plotted shapeliness of fiction, there are some points of interest in both stories. Each shows a person deeply depressed by the circumstances of their life and desperately seeking a resolution of an overwhelming problem. Each resolves that problem – has it resolved for them might be a better way of expressing the matter – by a selective reading of the scriptures. Both persons read the relevant parts of the Bible in accordance with their own presuppositions and following a particular way of reading it.

These stories are brilliant examples of the principle of 'text plus reader plus hermeneutic plus situation equals interpretation'. Nobody reading Romans 13.13–14 would necessarily decide that the text meant celibacy, though somebody with an Augustinian past might well seize on the phrase 'make no provision for the flesh, to gratify its desires' and gladly abandon the pursuit of men or women for sexual pleasure. A sacramental notion of sexuality or of marriage would not make a reader interpret Romans 13.14 as a call to celibacy – except perhaps in the sense of 'chaste sex' meaning sexual pleasure within a stable relationship. But Augustine's past and his Manichean outlook formed his reading of that particular piece of Pauline instruction. As he was already reading Paul before he heard the voice, it is hardly surprising that he should open the book of Paul's letters and encounter didactic instruction. (When Paul is not talking about himself he is usually issuing orders about how everybody should behave.) It would be out of place here to offer an account of Augustine and desire, especially in relation to his mother Monica, or to analyze the *Confessions* in terms of Augustine's presentation of self as a set of idealized fictions. The problematic of reading remains however, whether applied to the Bible or to Augustine.

John Bunyan's reading of scripture is typically that of a Puritan in the second half of the seventeenth century. No specific text is cited as being the cause of Christian's despair, nor is one supplied to explain why he should seek guidance from others, but his state of mind reflects that of the period in relation to a specific reading of certain texts. This reading is made up of a selection of New Testament texts which represent people as sinners by nature, lost unless they repent and find salvation in trusting Christ, with special emphasis on his atoning death on the cross. It is the kind of reading of scripture which survives to some extent in modern evangelicalism and fundamentalism (I take these two terms to be overlapping and coterminous rather than equivalent). As a very highly selective reading of a limited portion of the New Testament, bolstered by allegorical selections from the Christian Old Testament, it is very much the product of the seventeenth century and the Puritan hermeneutic of scripture. Where Bunyan's allegory gains its great appeal beyond the narrow confines of an obsolete Puritanism is in its allegorical representations of Christian's struggle against all odds to reach the celestial City and the characters he meets on the way there. The quality of Bunyan's English is superb and the characters are memorably depicted.

The biblical text as a life-changing agent

Now the experience of life-changing encounters with texts or things read is neither unusual nor confined to religious contexts. It is part of the lived experience (*Erlebnis*) of human beings living in communal environments. Literature and writing, like all art, can produce encounters and disclosures which change people's lives. Rilke's poem about the archaic torso of Apollo which challenges its viewer, 'You must change your life (*Leben*)', says of sculpture what all art says: 'You must change.' Whether that command can be heard by the average viewer/reader/hearer, or is appropriate to their situation, is another matter. But not only art and artistic constructions challenge human beings to change, or make them profoundly discontented with the misery of their lives; any chance encounter with something (or somebody) other than oneself can have that effect. To limit my remarks to what is written (what is *said* can be just as life-threatening or enhancing) in order to keep within the limits of this chapter, it must be said that *reading is a dangerous thing*. It can harm your psychic health. It certainly can change your life. Of course, whether it does or not depends on your situation and *how* you read. The thing written need not be profound but because it is always *other* than oneself its alterity can penetrate consciousness and radically alter how one thinks, behaves or lives. A chance remark, a glimpsed graffito on a wall, a sentence on a page or in a book, a half-remembered line from an old song, or something much more substantial such as an argument in a book understood for the first time, a story, a novel, a biography, even a critical study of something (dare I say, a commentary on a classic text?) – any such encounter could be the means of changing one's life in ways impossible to predict before the experience. People who are always open to encounters with the other (perhaps the upper case *O*ther is justified here) will know from experience what I am talking about. However, situation and openness may not always be necessary, for there are times when something outside oneself may suddenly strike one in ways never anticipated and start a chain reaction of responses which may prove to be life-changing.

For many centuries in religious communities the Bible and other books (too many to be enumerated here) have been important vehicles for such encounters with the Other. Not only books, of course. Other people, the worshipping communities, icons and holy pictures, nature, and the rituals of specific sects, have all contributed to change and life-enhancement – not to mention all the negative aspects of such changes. In the contemporary world the Bible may not play the roles it once did, and with the decline of literacy so-called 'great' literature may not be as significant as it once was, but the written word still has a strong grip on people in spite of television, videos and films. It is still possible to respond to the ringing doorbell and encounter two tall young American men in suits offering advice from *The Book of Mormon* (the Bible in another form!) or be confronted by two plump middle-aged women armed with a Bible and Watchtower literature. The growth in Mormonism and the Jehovah's Witnesses movement in modern Britain confirms the continued impact of the written word on people who wish to change their lives. Although the sandwich-board figure has virtually disappeared from the streets, the pedestrian walkways and shopping malls of modern cities still afford opportunities for leafleting and the handing out of religious or secular propaganda. Colporteurs may have vanished from our culture, but the door-to-door seller of encyclopedias and other books is not unknown (especially among students in America). Also the mail order book clubs and other forms of selling and distributing literature are a distinctive feature of contemporary society.

All of these selling activities reflect cultures still dominated to some extent by the written word. They include good and bad uses of literacy and life-changing projects, and often represent the commercialization of cultural products. While the spiritual effects of literature may be regarded as its most important contribution to human culture, the manufacturing and commercial processes of book-making and distribution have always been part of the production of literacy. Bibles also are a money-generating enterprise, and the monopolies on printing the Bible held by ancient firms are a testimony not to spirituality but to commercial values. Hence the large number of *new* translations of the Bible as every publisher attempts to corner part of the market for one of the world's outstanding bestsellers (the Bible as commodity). Printing Bibles is as much a political and commercial activity as it is anything else. The more negative aspects of literary influence I shall not attempt to delineate here as they are not really part of my concern in this chapter. Also I am aware of the value judgements involved in deciding such matters and the relativity of all such opinions – one person's Mede is another person's Persian!

For me the real problematic of reading the Bible and taking it seriously in relation to one's own life is constituted by the tensions between how one might interpret a specific part of it and all the contextual, situational, existential and historical issues which bear on any such reading. Remembering my remarks on the infantilism inherent in the attempts of 'biblical Christianity' movements to skip over nearly two thousand years of history in order to bring together two discrete epochs – that of the Bible and that of contemporary society – I am deeply aware of how problematic any application of the Bible to modern life can be. Also, it is not possible to read the Bible as if one were coming to it for the first time and without any consciousness of centuries of inculturation involving Bible, churches/synagogues, and Western civilization. We hear the Bible now (or read it individually) as an iconic book out of the past of our culture. There are so many factors implicit in any approach to the Bible that it really is extremely difficult to imagine that what one is doing when reading it is encountering it without complex considerations mediating its meaning to us. For example, absolutely no Christian reader is going to read the book of Leviticus *as it stands* and be conscience-stricken because they are not regularly sacrificing sheep and goats. Christian readers will respond to this objection: 'That is not *how* you read Leviticus. You must read the Old Testament in the light of what the New Testament has to say about the death of Jesus *as a sacrifice*.' Leviticus is to be read historically, typologically (christologically) and allegorically, but not as divine commands for modern readers.

The cluster of problems inherent in that controlling of the text by other texts – equivalent to allowing the commentary to pre-empt the text and substitute its meaning for the text's meaning – is one part of the problematic. Texts which confront readers with the demand to change their lives are not texts which can be defused in such a secondary manner. The reinterpreted text loses much of its force and becomes domesticated. Its wildness and rawness are sacrificed to comfortable exegesis. That, of course, is the nature of texts which have endured over time: they survive because they are capable of (almost) infinite reinterpretation. It is the *rewritten* text which comes down through time, rather than the original form. The translated Bible – that is, the Bible mediated through time by changing language shifts – is what the reader encounters. Translated and interpreted – a double translation – and controlled by prevailing canons of exegesis and concomitant hermeneutic principles, the Bible we read today is a mere shadow and echo of books people once found life-changing.

In choosing an example from Leviticus I deliberately picked one from the boundary rather than what many readers of the Bible might regard as a more central text. In this book I am not working with centre-periphery notions of the biblical text, nor am I operating with time-honoured concepts such as 'the canon within the canon' principle. These are modes which have the net effect of escaping the text in order to preserve selected parts of it. The problematic which concerns me has to do with the *whole* Bible – be it Hebrew, Christian or Protestant. Once the principle is accepted that we may shift the significance of a text into a new hermeneutic mode, then texts lose their power to challenge us or to confront us with life-changing possibilities. The text is disarmed and made safe for domestic consumption. While the practice of reinterpreting texts is inevitable in order to update ancient literature or to make it fit the social structures into which it has been incorporated, there is such a loss of force and integrity that books such as the Bible quickly become cripples in the community. This savaging of the Bible can be understood in a dialectical manner so as to save something of its wildness. We may say that the retention of the Bible – or parts within it – allows it to function as a voice from the past as well as a voice updated in modern language. Whether the tension is genuinely dialectical or just paradoxical is a moot point. Much of modern theology which is thought of as being dialectical is more often confused, equivocal or paradoxical, rather than dialectical at all. Dialectical is a good old-fashioned philosophical (Socratic) term which is used to give theological thought a good pedigree and to give body to ageing and tired theological concepts. Updating the interpretation of the Bible while allowing the 'original' (i.e. translated) words to have some force may only produce irresolvable tensions.

A different example may be chosen from the material in Matthew 5—7 which is popularly known as the 'Sermon on the Mount'. There are so many different instructions in these chapters which sit so uneasily with modern bourgeois religious life. They constitute a good sample of 'change your life' assertions. The modern Christian living in a fine four-floor house with two mortgages and two cars, regular holidays abroad, with the average number of children in the family, fashionably dressed, an assiduous attender at public worship every week, and an upstanding member of the community with a good public reputation, must read Matthew 5—7 and shiver. The practice of praying in public is also denounced:

When you pray, you must not be like the hypocrites; for they love to stand and pray in the synagogues and at the street corners, that they may be seen by men. Truly, I say to you, they have received their reward. But when you pray, go into your room and shut the door and pray to your Father who is in secret; and your Father who sees in secret will reward you. (Matt. 6.5-6)

Anyone who has witnessed a charismatic meeting where people were standing and dancing and praying and praising in the most ostentatious of ways will instantly call to mind those words attributed to Jesus. I do not doubt that charismatic forms of worship can be defended on various grounds, including New Testament texts about glossolalia, but the text which bites and says 'change your life' is the one in Matthew 6.5-6. Those who have ears to hear let them hear!

Other elements in the so-called 'Sermon on the Mount' are equally disparaging of bourgeois developments in the Christian religion. The prohibition against 'laying up for yourselves treasures on earth, where moth and rust consume and where thieves break in and steal' (Matt. 6.19) is only partially frustrated by modern banking systems. It speaks against any Christian who has a bank account or shares or accumulated wealth and property. The lengthy section in Matthew 6.25-34 speaks much about having no possessions and more about having no anxiety about the morrow. It is one of the great, almost Stoic, texts of the New Testament. But in modern culture with its notions of careful planning of the future down to the fine detail of insurance policies, pension schemes, the making of wills and deferred payments, taking thought for the morrow and planning for it are a way of life. That is just how modernity has rendered the ancient texts obsolete. The embourgeoisement of Christianity (I use a modern word here to represent what can be discerned as happening in some of the shorter letters in the New Testament itself as well as the more general modernization of ancient religion in recent centuries) may have been the inevitable consequence of the successes the early churches had over the centuries, especially after Constantine. Any religion which successfully outgrows its origins – as all religions must do if they are to survive at all – will have to reinterpret, ignore or allegorize its past in order to maintain a good conscience. But if the texts remain on the books as it were, then problems can arise, and voices from the past will whisper to solitary readers, 'You must change your life.'

I do not wish to be thought a complete simpleton in this matter, but an important point is being made about the Bible. Because it comes from other ages the ways of life reflected in it are very different from the ways we live now in the West. Other parts of the world will still find the social world of the Bible a place to be at home in. That is why in recent years liberation theology has been able to make such headway in various countries other than in the West. There is a directness about what is said in the Bible which speaks straight to the social environment of poor people who have neither great possessions nor any prospects beyond getting through each day one at a time. Obsolete in the West, the Bible lives on in other parts of the world. Sophisticated theologians and biblical exegetes will produce many different hermeneutics to explain why a literal understanding of the 'Sermon on the Mount' is not to be entertained by the reader. I know that reading consists of text plus hermeneutic plus situation plus reader, and that therefore any modern reading of Matthew 5—7 must inevitably change so many things as to render the original text beyond our grasp. That is the central problem of reading the Bible today. Time and fortune have swept it away in a stream of reinterpreted readings so that it no longer has bite or bark (if I may mix metaphors somewhat). Exposed to centuries of pietistic interpretation and of accommodation to changing circumstances, the book is now part of the problem (whether it was ever, outside reformed circles, part of the solution is quite another question) and I cannot think of a way to resolve that problem which does not entail creating even greater problems.

Among the sophisticated moves which an exegete might make when dealing with the 'Sermon on the Mount' are such framing approaches as treating the material as 'interim ethics'. That is, the rules in the Sermon (Matthew 5—7 is of course a construction of the Gospel writer and not the reportage of an actual sermon preached by Jesus; a scrutiny of the other Gospels will demonstrate the truth of this observation) were designed to be practised by the early Christians until the return of Jesus brought the age to an end. The delay of that return (*parousia*) and the eventual loss of belief in such an event, except as a figure for the end of time, rendered the ethics irrelevant and inappropriate for well-developed and rapidly-changing communities. Jesus and Paul both appear to have shared the expectation of the end of the world as an imminent occurrence – I know it is unwise to infer from statements in the Gospels what the historical Jesus might have believed, but there are many sayings in the Gospels which make better sense as reflections of a belief in the imminent end of the world than they do of any alternative explanation. Paul makes arbitrary rulings which are grounded in his conviction that 'the appointed time has grown very short' (e.g. 1 Cor. 7.25–40; the cited phrase appears in verse 29). Such matters are subject to the corrections of time and circumstance. As 'interim ethics' the commandments of the 'Sermon on the Mount' would have no validity beyond the first or second century and so modern wealthy Christians are off the hook!

An alternative explanation of the regulations of the 'Sermon on the Mount' would be to treat them not as rules but as counsels of perfection. The instruction is given to the disciples (Matt. 5.1) and so concerns the inner community of the faithful, the élite. As such it is intended to outline the values of the inner group and to provide guidelines for the perfecting of the spiritual life of those who follow the path of discipleship. Being a disciple involves a life dedicated to becoming what in later times would be called a saint. So the 'Sermon' does not concern the ordinary believer – if such a distinction existed in the mind of Jesus or of the Gospel writer – but seekers after perfection. This is an explanation of sorts, but it seems to presuppose too many things about the Gospel and the social world of the early Christians to make for a good reading of the text. The close reader of Matthew 5—7 will notice that by the time the writer has brought the 'Sermon' to an end, Jesus is described as teaching 'the crowds' (7.28–29; *hoi hochloi* could be translated as 'the mobs'). There are also various instructions within the 'Sermon' which are better understood as differentiating between those who would be disciples and those who are not.

Luther's notion of the 'Sermon' as expressing the thesis that such ideals cannot be put into practice and that therefore the 'Sermon' is intended to make plain to hearer and reader the impossibility of such 'good works' belongs to his ideology of 'faith versus good works' and is alien to the Gospels. It is, however, a good example of yet another way people have read the 'Sermon' in order to make sense of it in relation to their own beliefs, practices and hermeneutic. What does appear to be the case with all the differing approaches to reading Matthew 5—7 (and there are many more which I have not considered here) is the strong recognition of the problematics of *reading* involved in the text. While my own approach to the 'Sermon' favours the 'interim ethics' framework of interpretation, I have to recognize that every reading of the text has problems. It is the survival of the 'Sermon' in the canon of scripture which makes it so problematic for modern interpretations, because canonic writings invariably operate as normative material in communities which recognize such writings as canonical.

I am not at all sure that using the 'Sermon on the Mount' as an example of the problematic of reading the Bible straight (i.e. without benefit of a mediating hermeneutic, just as one would read a classic or modern novel) is any more problem-free than reading the book of Leviticus straight. Allowing the text to exercise constraints on the reader makes it difficult to subject it to an accommodating hermeneutic. Reading the Gospels' representation of Jesus without benefit of the critical approach to reading biblical texts – an unwise move because it quickly becomes evident that some such criticality is required to deal with contradictions, inconsistencies and other problems in the text – it is possible to discern, perhaps rather dimly at times, a stark, uncompromising figure akin to a wild Hebrew prophet; a figure ranged against every manner of authority, both social and religious, and implacably opposed to the politics of family, home and conformity. It is true that this figure is regularly overladen with elements from different portrayals: he behaves almost like a rabbi at times, conforming to whatever information the Gospel writer may have had about such Jewish figures. On this point it must be said that while the essential Jewishness of Jesus can hardly be questioned, it is far from clear that all the Gospel writers were well informed about Jewish practice in the time of Jesus. For example, where does Matthew get the notion that the synagogue was a place for standing up in and praying (6.5)? Christians should not be like hypocrites (Jewish hypocrites I suppose, for who else would go to synagogues?), but would Jesus have known such synagogues where great play-acting went into public prayers? Is there not an element of chauvinistic criticism of other people's imagined or pejoratively reported religion involved here? But that is the critical spirit reviewing the text rather than going with the flow of it. Clearly I find it hard to enter into the first/second century writer's mind without abandoning the late-twentieth-century mind only in part. That is always a problem of reading ancient texts and trying to overcome the fact that texts always have several epochs to them.

Extrapolating the figure of a Jewish prophet from the Gospels as a possible glimpse of the original Jesus – for reasons too many to list here I think the various forms of the quest for the historical Jesus are doomed to failure – I find other texts keep interfering with this image. A wandering, charismatic miracle-worker who speaks as a prophet is one thing. But such a figure who gets invited to dinner at the houses of Pharisees or whose teaching is such that Pharisees and teachers of *torah* flock to hear him from every village of Galilee and Judea *and from Jerusalem* (!) makes one abandon the prophet hypothesis (cf. Luke 5.17). And yet the wildness of that figure does capture an important element in the representation of Jesus which I am loath to let go just in order to reconcile the irreconcilabilities of the Gospels. It fits those bits of teaching which speak out against the bourgeois domesticities (I cannot think of a more historically accurate or appropriate word than 'bourgeois') to be found creeping into the Gospels at certain points and which are characteristic of the long history of the Christian reception of Jesus. It is this wild figure who speaks out against the accumulation of wealth and the shoring up of securities against the future. This appears to be the Jesus who calls people to follow him, to give up everything and to take up their crosses and face death with him.

It is this Jesus as a rootless, footloose, wandering prophet which comes across from a carefully filtered and filleted reading of the Gospels. The image is enhanced by the following story:

> As they were going along the road, a man said to him, 'I will follow you wherever you go.' And Jesus said to him, 'Foxes have holes, and birds of the air have nests; but the Son of man has nowhere to lay his head.' To another he said, 'Follow me.' But he said, 'Lord, let me first go and bury my father.' But he said to him, 'Leave the dead to bury their own dead; but as for you, go and proclaim the kingdom of God.' Another said, 'I will follow you, Lord; but let me first say farewell to those at my home.' Jesus said to him, 'No one who puts his hand to the plough and looks back is fit for the kingdom of God.' (Luke 9.57–61; cf. Matt. 8.19–22)

Whatever the Gospel writer has added to or done with the original material in that pericope, the figure in the text is still that of a person profoundly opposed to familial loyalties. The image of one who is homeless and rootless is striking. What makes it particularly striking is the contrast between it and the subsequent lifestyles of so many Christians. The modern *soi-disant* disciples of Jesus are often people of whom it cannot be said that they are homeless; on the contrary they are frequently people of more than one home/house. I know there are many disciples who have taken vows of poverty and who are genuine followers of the homeless Son of man. I also am aware that down through the centuries of Christendom there have been orders of monks and communities of nuns who have taken most seriously their discipleship in terms of poverty, chastity and obedience. The world is still full of such people. Umberto Eco's famous novel *The Name of the Rose* includes some scintillating discussions of the medieval heresy – at least it became a heresy once the Catholic Church pronounced officially on it – that Jesus had no possessions and that therefore Christians should have none either. Such a literal *imitatio Christi* was reckoned to be too subversive of a Church much given to wealth and possessions, so orthodoxy was defined to include the belief that Jesus had had possessions.

My final illustration of texts which demand of you that 'you must change your life' must be taken from the one central narrative of the Gospels. Untainted by later dogma but complicated by the narratological modes of representation used by all the Gospel writers – and the inevitable post-resurrection influences of the early churches' reading of the life of Jesus – the story of the seizure, trial, inquisition and execution of Jesus on the hill of Golgotha (note how the Latinity of the word 'Calvary' softens and threatens to domesticate the harshness of that hard word 'Golgotha') allows the point to be made. I shall not dwell on the central icon of the Christian faith. The details are too well known to bear repetition and the story itself has often been lost under a welter of dogmatic theologizing. The Roman state authorities crucified Jesus along with other criminals. I daresay they had the co-operation of some Jewish authorities, especially the religious ones. We know from Josephus – how reliable a writer he was is an open question – that in the first century conflicting interests among Jews could make their internecine struggles very vicious affairs. Crucifixion was a degrading and cruel punishment and there is no reason to think that the Roman executioners were Christian gentlemen of an idealistic temperament. It is however one of the most curious – and unpleasant I think – features of most of the New Testament writings (the Apocalypse is a notable exception) that they are such apologists for the Roman *imperium*. *Realpolitik* I suppose. As represented in the Gospels the execution of Jesus is a striking critique of political structures. All the interests come together, and various political factions co-operate in killing – a judicial killing at that (i.e. after benefit of Roman trial) and not a lynching – the wild prophet from the provinces (or 'sticks' as we might say today). The crucified Jew readily becomes a symbol for the downtrodden peasant and ethnic minority caught in the maelstrom of power politics and imperial arrogance. He also, unfortunately, presages a long history to come of slaughtered Jews. There is a fellowship of the crucified Jew which has little or nothing to do with Christian values or institutions, and which inevitably catches the mind of the competent reader of the Gospels who is perforce familiar with nearly two thousand years of history (see the crucifixion paintings of Chagall).

What the story of the resurrection of Jesus does to the story I have outlined in the preceding paragraph I do not know. In the New Testament it appears to transform everything, but that appearance may be a case of rushing to judgement. Mark's Gospel states the 'fact' (if fact it is, then it is of a different order of facts from those which pertain to the material world of history and human habitation) of the resurrection and leaves it to resonate among the women who are fearful (Mark 16.1–8). Other Gospels are less reticent. The triumphalism of the preaching (*kerygma*) of the early churches may be seen in the book of Acts and the writings of Paul. That rather triumphalist transformation of the wild prophet's anti-bourgeois preaching and outsider's death at the hands of powerful interests will with time and the influx of many other influences give rise to the mighty state organization of the Catholic Church, and the fist will be in the other glove. Theologians trained in the subtleties of substantive philosophy will combine with other factors to transform biblical images and metaphors into theological dogmas which will recast the Jewish prophet into the second person of the most Holy Trinity. That orthodoxy will form the oppositional backdrop to the quest for fidelity to what will survive of the vision of the Galilean preacher.

I am deeply aware that my reading of the text has quickly become an interpretation, assisted by information external to the text and a hermeneutic determined by complex factors not entirely derived from the text. That is part of the problem of reading the New Testament today. Two thousand years of development, reinterpretation and the acquisitions of newer hermeneutic skills make the story almost impossible to read *as if* for the first time. Such *as if* readings are difficult for the modern mind, especially one so heavily influenced by so many transformations of the story in the first place. The ecclesiastical domestications of the story over the centuries have rendered it inert within the dogmatic system which controls all readings of it. Readings from outside the churches cannot penetrate the protective devices employed by the institutions and, besides, their proprietary rights over the story make them constitutionally deaf to alternative readings. My reading cannot handle the transcendental dimensions of what the resurrection does to the already highly interpreted (in the text) story in the Gospels. This side of Auschwitz I find the resurrection a profoundly puzzling tale which I can only deal with in terms of symbolic forms. The starker story of the betrayal, seizure, trial and execution I can begin to read and understand because it chimes in with the long tale of human history with its subtext of suffering and oppression.

Linking this final example from the Gospels with the representation of the Christian churches in the world today, I find many questions surface in my reading of the ancient texts. Observing various high dignitaries of the churches parading about in their splendid robes and presiding over rituals of astounding beauty and deep symbolic values, I wonder what possible connections can any of it have with the story of an executed Jewish peasant so many centuries ago. How can such wealth, power and position be a necessary manifestation of the call of discipleship which entails no property, no money, no power (except of a different dimension), but which evokes a fellowship of suffering and crucifixion? Are the transformations from poverty as discipleship to wealth and bourgeois respectability legitimate translations of the ancient call to follow? Have they been legitimated through time and the necessary adjustments for developmental processes whereby changing customs have replaced older outworn values? I ask these questions because they seem to me to be involved in any reading of these biblical texts in the light of the historical developments of the many diverse movements which constituted the early churches. I find it very difficult to equate that figure bleeding and hanging from a Roman gibbet as a result of the machinations of political and religious power interests with the formal activities of such splendiferously robed figures as, say, the Archbishop of Canterbury or the Pope. Of course I shall be told that the resurrection makes all the difference. The figure no longer hangs from a cross but is enthroned in power and the churches represent him – nay, are him – on earth. I find that tale even worse than my reading of the Gospels. For if the churches are the body of Christ on earth – a metaphor to be found in the New Testament but not in the Gospels – then all that long history of persecution and antisemitism is but the activity of Christ himself on earth. That is frightening beyond words.

That then is the problem of reading the Gospels in the light of history and making due allowance for hermeneutic sophistication. It is equally the problem of trying to read them without allowing factors other than the text to influence one's reading. I have probably demonstrated that it is simply not possible to read ancient religious texts – or at least the Bible which is a special case – *as if* for the first time. Nor is it feasible to try to read the Bible *as if* there had not been a long history of its production and a longer history of its reinterpretation through many different epochs. Yet it is the Gospel story, whichever one is chosen, which approximates to the cultural object which says, 'You must change your life', rather than the long history of its reception. Some readers may feel that it is still possible to be open enough to read the Gospels and to respond to them in life-changing ways. I daresay it is. There are many examples of people within and outside of all the churches who find it possible to change their lives through their reading of the Bible. The same may be said about the Hebrew Bible (*mutatis mutandis*). A reading of Amos or of Qoheleth could waken anybody from their dogmatic slumbers. Mind you, I can also foresee such awakened people being chased out of churches, synagogues or other meeting-places of the guardians of sacred scripture!

The taming of the Bible

The encounter with the biblical text which is capable of making the reader wish to change how one's life is lived is a possibility which every cultural artefact may engender in any encounter with it. What militates against such encounters is the comfortability of culture in our time. In religious circles the Bible has been domesticated or compromised by religious lunatics or hi-jacked by pressure groups whose interests alienate ordinary people. In so many different ways the wildness inherent in the interstices of the book has been tamed by over-exposure or over-use. Kafka's notion of a book as an 'axe' might be applied to various books in the Bible, but who among its readers would wish to have their skulls split open by their sacred book? The title of this chapter, 'Wolf in Sheep's Clothing' is meant to convey to the reader something of Kafka's demands of books that

they should terrify us and shock us in order to unfreeze our insides –
what a powerful and percipient reader of scripture Franz Kafka was.
The phrase is of course taken from Matthew's 'Sermon on the
Mount', where in talking about false prophets Jesus is represented as
saying, 'Beware of false prophets, who come to you in sheep's
clothing but inwardly are ravenous wolves' (7.15; the saying only
occurs in Matthew's Gospel). The rapacious wolf (inward state) in
sheep's clothing (outward appearance) is a graphic image of the
effects of what is false (the pseudoprophets). It is a very characteristic
biblical notion of the distinction between appearance and reality.
I have therefore appropriated it for this book because it nicely plots
the gap between how people see the Bible and what it really contains
(i.e. its subtext). Among the sheep (i.e. in the sheepfold) it appears as
a sheep but *at heart* it is (or to be more accurate it *contains* within its
multitudinous parts) a rapacious wolf. Like Kafka's notion of the
books we need, the Bible too can affect us like a disaster, a death, a
suicide, and it too can be an axe breaking up the frozen sea of our
hearts and minds. If I may adapt verses which in some religious
circles are often used of the Bible but which appear in the Bible with
rather a different sense: on the right occasion the bit of the Bible we
may happen to be reading can be like the divine word which is
described as a fire and a hammer (Jer. 23.29) or as being sharper than
a two-edged sword (Heb. 4.12). I prefer the figure of the rapacious
wolf, especially if it comes under the guise of a sheep; but of course
the biblical writers did not know a Bible so could not have used the
imagery of a collection of books.

No irony is intended in my use of the phrases 'wolf in the
sheepfold' and 'wolf in sheep's clothing' to draw attention to certain
aspects of the Bible for theology. I dare say some readers will find
such uses rather ironic – irony is often in the ear of the beholder! –
and there may be some mileage in the notion that it is perhaps
(highly?) ironic that the Bible (parts of it) should be seen today as
constituting a rapacious animal within the communities which
produced it (a version of it) and have long cherished it. But
alternative views of the Bible *as a serious book* tend to treat it with
reverential deference and to domesticate it. Its functions as fetish and
commodity, idol and desire, tend to reduce it to the status of a 'sheep
in wolf's clothing'. Superficially it looks dangerous but underneath it
is gentle and amenable to all the different ways religious communities
handle it. It does not scare or terrify; it does not threaten or upset. It

would never scare the horses in the street or disturb the mighty in their seats. Millionaire evangelists can ply their wares from the Bible without having to worry about biblical denunciations of wealth or false prophets. Of course there are many parts of the Bible which applaud wealth and prophecy, so I am only focusing on the awkward parts of the collection. The bits which interest me in this book are those which get under your fingernails and cause great pain – those irritating sayings and sections which disturb the mind and rob you of your sleep at night; the parts which sit uneasily with doctrine and dogma and which mock the domesticities of religions which swear by the Bible. Bunyan's Christian figure at least seemed to be upset ('devastated' would be *le mot juste*) by the reading of the book, for axe-like it broke through his complacency and forced him to act on what he was reading. It killed him and brought him back to life on another level. It is that 'naught for your comfort' (to use Chesterton's phrase) aspect of the book which poses the problem for the pious reader of the book.

In a short book of exploratory sketches it is not possible to do justice to every viewpoint or to map accurately the world of Bible readers and users. Generalizations are inevitable, and also are rather vulnerable to piecemeal rebuttal by a thousand instances of differences in beliefs and practices about the Bible. The generality of my remarks is intended to capture something of the puzzlement that some theologically minded people express about how the Bible can be used in the churches today, and to map out some of my own reflections and observations on the Bible as a problem for theology. It is when I see a television evangelist demand money 'in the name of Jesus' while waving a rather large Bible at people that I realize what a huckster religion some forms of Christianity have become. Do these sellers of religion to the masses never read the New Testament? Have they ever read Matthew's 'Sermon on the Mount'? What kind of reading of the Bible is it that produces this kind of bazaar? Do they not know the early writings of the churches which produced rules governing prophets and charismatics (the *Didache*), regulations which include the identification of the false prophet as the one who asks for money? Readers may object that such people are only 'telly goons' and are not representative of the mainstream churches or of the mass of godly Christians. In my opinion they are more representative than people on this side of the Atlantic often imagine and, furthermore, many of their beliefs, especially about the Bible, are shared by many in Europe. In fact, some of these evangelists (television and otherwise) are warmly invited to visit Britain and hold campaigns to evangelize on a mass scale. Such hucksters may sell the Bible short but there are many buyers of their wares.

The less wild shores of biblicist evangelization campaigns have been equally well-known since the days of the famous Moody and Sankey revival meetings of the last century. We are all familiar with this type of American import (Moody and Sankey made their mark on Glasgow in the 1890s), and especially since the 1940s with the Billy Graham campaigns. Most of these gatherings are relatively harmless (though psychiatrists often tell a different story) because they are very much forms of entertainment which tend to church the already churched or to bring back to the churches lapsed members. Perhaps they are not designed to be so domestic, but that seems to be their main achievement. Such uses of the Bible reflect a domestication of the wildness of its parts and are invariably contextualized socially in terms of lower middle class, or somewhat bourgeois, values. This is the Bible as a sheep in wolf's clothing. The savage critique of religiosity and religious leaders, of politicians and the state, of the family and wealth, so characteristic of parts of the Bible (e.g. the prophets, the 'Sermon on the Mount') is ignored in favour of an anodyne mixture of biblical rhetoric and social respectability. A nineteenth-century pietism is combined with the social values of the preacher and together they are equated with the gospel. This gospel is then proclaimed as the answer to life's problems as if it were a new shampoo or the latest fashion in deodorant. The religious package is marketed as a consumerist product and sold to all comers. And that is how the Bible becomes domesticated in such circles.

A similar critique of such meetings has been made by Darrel Robertson in his study of the 1876 Chicago Revival which was generated by Moody and Sankey. If I quote Robertson's concluding paragraph it will indicate an interesting critique of some of the social consequences of that campaign and will contribute to my own criticisms of this type of evangelistic selling of bourgeois values:

The Chicago revival also points up the sometimes intimate relation of religion with ethnic and class identities. This should be of little surprise since people seem naturally to seek community with their own kind, with those who share similar values and interpretations of the ultimate meaning of life. The revival of 1876 tended to enhance this sense of community for middle-class, Anglo-American, white city dwellers. Its rhetoric, in fact, sacralized certain middle-class social and moral conceptions, *bestowing upon them an aura of ultimate and universal validity.* While the purpose of this essay has been to examine and assess the significance of Moody and the revival in Chicago and not to make pejorative judgements, it seems appropriate to observe *the danger inherent in too readily identifying cultural values with absolute truth.* If their violent denunciations of the social habits of immigrants or the labor unrest of 1877 be adequate indication, revival Chicagoans were little able or willing to bridge with sensitivity or understanding the cultural chasm between themselves and the immigrant and laboring poor of the city. *They had,* perhaps unwittingly, *made the New Testament Christ of the poor, hungry, and socially outcast into a sentimental, moralistic, legalistic, and middle-class Savior of the 1870s.* (*emphases added*)

Now before the reader thinks that I am indulging in the very old sport of 'knocking the bourgeoisie', I must insist that the point I am labouring concerns the great gulf fixed between the Jesus of the Gospels and the Christ preached by modern bourgeois church people. There is nothing inherently wrong with being middle-class, peasant, underclass or whatever social stratum one may assign oneself to. Academics are necessarily middle-class, but this is not an attack on the class to which I now belong. It is very much an introductory study of the problem of the Bible as it appears when modern religious uses of it are contrasted with what the text says. The Jesus figure detectable behind the many representations of him by the Gospel writers is clearly not a primitive middle-class character. He is Jewish for a start! Apparently he is also illegitimate (how the legends of Matthew 1—2 and Luke 1—2 should be related to any *reliable* information about his parentage is both a matter of interpretation and of controversy) and a provincial. He also appears to be somewhat footloose, perhaps even a charismatic and some kind of miracle-worker; possibly he could be described as a prophet, and he may be a little mad (lunacy is a relative and socially constructed term). Given to violent outbursts of temper, he could be very aggressive ('hooligan' is a contemporary term which would be applied to such provincials - even perhaps 'wine lout', cf. John 2.1-11; Matt. 11.19; Luke 7.34) and seems not to have respected property (Matt. 21.12-13; Mark 11.15-17; Luke 19.45-46; John 2.13-16) or family (e.g. Mark 3.31-35; Luke 2.41-49; John 2.4). However one describes this person or the teaching attributed to him, the word which does *not* come to mind is bourgeois.

On the other hand, when one listens to the public declarations of Christians in the West today, or reads the destroyed forests of books and pamphlets put out by the Christian churches, the messages are invariably bourgeois. Pressure groups and political lobbies mushroom throughout the land in favour of marriage and sex *after* marriage (and only *within* the confines of monogamous relationships), and advocate all the values of lower-middle-class standards for everybody. To hear such people speaking is to be deluded into thinking that various forms of Christianity have as their sole purpose the imposition of middle-class values on the nations. I know that such concerns have steadily become the preoccupation of many Christian communities since the eighteenth century and are not to be confused, for one moment, with ancient Christian values – though I must admit that there are some signs of the embourgeoisement of the churches in some of the minor writings in the New Testament. Socially, Christian ethics seem always to have gravitated to the respectable end of the social spectrum, and this shift contrasts spectacularly with the preaching of the kingdom associated with Jesus. The proclamation of chastity and poverty would be more in keeping with discipleship of Jesus, but that would hardly make the gospel the cultural property of the middle classes. So my point about the problem of reading the Bible and taking it to heart has to do with the stark contrast between *some* of the things written in the New Testament and the way the churches have developed over many centuries.

The radical transformations by the churches, over nearly two millennia, of the gospel of the kingdom preached by the vagrant Galilean prophet are hardly surprising given the many different influences which have contributed to the formation of historical Christianity. Constantly changing circumstances and ideologies forged a very distinctive kind of religion which in turn eventually gave rise to many of the churches which flourish (or otherwise) in the contemporary world. The primitive gospel was always subject to change, and like a chrysalis – a series of chrysalises would be more accurate – has become something rather different in the fullness of time. The only problem with this development is that the ancient books have been preserved along with all the changes, and remain there like wasps in amber. As vestiges of ancient times these books have an abiding interest for the antiquarian and those of a historical bent of mind. At a pinch they might be regarded as voices from the past with the potential for becoming occasionally *criticism from the past*. The old ways and standards might still have something to say to the modern mind and might even contribute something to the very necessary creation of a critique of ideology (*Ideologiekritik*). Our easy activisms, our love of dressing up in fashionable costumes, and all the paraphernalia of contemporary religious observances might still benefit from the shock of contemplating the old. The vision of the naked Christ, dressed only in the robe provided by his own blood, mocks our gaudy rituals devoted to the idols of our tamed religions. The books might still have some juice left in them. But none of this is the problem of the Bible as focused on by this chapter. It is the insistence that the books remain what they were thought to be so many centuries ago which undermines the various transformational developments of the churches and poses the problem of reading them today. How can they be read *as if* nothing had ever happened between their being written and where we are now?

My notion of the problem goes deeper. Taking as my model the art object (book, painting, song, poem, sculpture, dance, play, symphony, etc.) which confronts its observer with the challenge, 'You must change your life', I feel that taking the books of the Bible seriously may also induce such a challenge. That indictment of life and command to change generated by a part of the Bible problematizes the religious control of the book. For the change may well be away from all one's cherished notions of religious commitment and the long-established meaning of texts to a way of life at odds with conventional values. Imagine if you will a preacher, on reading the Bible carefully, renouncing the dogmas of the Christian faith because they are not to be found in scripture! Conceive of that speaker as giving up a well-paid job in order to seek life at a different level. How catastrophic it could be for church structures if too many people, never mind just preachers, ministers and priests, started to find life outside the religious structures. The problem arises out of the tensions created by the subsumption of the ancient books into transformed belief systems. Those systems militate against any exposure to things which threaten to ruin conventional life with insistent demands for serious change.

This chapter is *not* advocating biblicism or any form of fundamentalist reading of the Bible. Nor is it seeking to encourage an infantile retreat to the past or a futile return to infancy. What it is trying to get a bite on is the notion of the Bible as literature. As a collection of different and discrete books it brings together many occasions for encounters with a literary object which may function in the ways outlined by Kafka and Rilke at the beginning of this chapter. It is not the Bible *in toto* which constitutes the literary entity, but the various books (or parts of books) within whichever version the reader favours. Thus a reading of Job, Jonah, Qoheleth, Amos, Song of Solomon, Ruth, Romans, Mark or James might occasion change in the reader's life. Then again it might not. The encounter with texts which changes lives is a subtle blend of reader, situation, text, reading and occasion. It is governed by time and chance as much as by other factors and can never be guaranteed. Readers have to be ready for texts and have to be found by texts. Who can arrange such things!

The problematic arises out of the fact that the Bible is not just any collection of books. It is also the canonic scriptures of various religious communities and is therefore built into a nexus of many other forms of life. As such its capacity for life-changing possibilities may be severely restricted. How it functions and what it means are already prescribed for it and any individual encounter with it must occur outside such structures of culturally determined religions. So the problematic may be resolved quite easily by removing the Bible from the category of 'reading this book can damage your health/ change your life' books. As a religious book (now) the Bible escapes from being literature. Or as the poet Auden put it: 'Thou shalt not be on friendly terms/With guys in advertising firms,/Nor speak with such/As read the Bible for its prose.'

Conclusion

State the facts,
Read the text right, emancipate the world –
The emancipated world enjoys itself
With scarce a thank you . . .

Robert Browning

My brief trawls through a number of examples of the Bible as a problem are over. I must leave to the reader the decision as to whether these exploratory samples are representative of a benign or malign condition of the Bible. If the Bible is really so much a problem for Christianity, and specifically for theology, would it not be better for theology to abandon the book altogether? That is certainly one possibility. On the other hand, the Bible comes to us out of the past and is one of the links with ancient roots which communities have long cherished. As a reservoir of images and metaphors it still offers readers a wide range of generative possibilities. It contains stories which are not only timeless, but which have shaped how we think and feel about the world and other things. The very long history of its reception has added to that shaping influence. Who could fail to benefit from reading the great readers of scripture such as Origen, Augustine, Aquinas, Calvin or Barth, not to mention all the poets and writers whose work may fall outside ecclesiastical domains? Read in conjunction with the history of its interpretation, the Bible can be a powerful contributor to the formation of sensibility and insight. It is difficult to explain its formative power because how each person reads a story and reflects on it varies from person to person. Familiarization with biblical narratives and poems develops a feel for a certain kind of storytelling and an appreciation of ironic understatement. Biblical rhetoric once formed part of the English language, though much of that has disappeared now in our post-literate culture. But these are all reflections on the Bible *as literature* and do not touch its problematic status for theology.

Theology can survive with or without the Bible. The churches are not going to be affected one way or another by the fact that the Bible

144

complicates their theology or even undermines it. They have survived far too long for that to be a problem. Such communities have developed strategies for reading the Bible which chime in with their theologies. That has always been the great strength of canons of scripture. They underwrite so many different, and often contradictory, systems of thought and are amenable to endless interpretative conceits. The reader's role in interpreting the Bible can relativize it with no difficulty. As William Blake observed about different visions of Christ (mine and thine): 'Both read the Bible day and night,/But thou read'st black where I read white.'

Where the problematic may disturb people is in a context of aspiring to combine Bible and theology into a consistent, coherent system of thought. This is where the different natures of the two entities – Bible and theology – are at war with each other. They are at war because their roots are different and the ways they generate thought very distinctive. Pulling and tugging biblical metaphors kicking and screaming into a theological system can be the death of the biblical imagery. However, theological systems are not usually that crude and tend to operate with subtler uses of the Bible as illustrations of theology or as starting-points for the development of theological concepts. Sometimes these approaches work quite well, but they misfire when reversed so as to read the Bible *as if* the biblical writers also used the words and concepts in the same way. The arrow of time flies only in one direction and while the theological method may co-opt biblical terms and notions to *serve* a particular system, these biblical elements cannot be thought of as being interchangeable with the developing theology. This would be to make religion ahistorical, and the Bible a filing-cabinet of abstract ideas.

The critical reading of the Bible has often been seen as hostile to theology. On the contrary, it is perhaps the first stage in the development of a seriously critical theology. If criticism and theology appear to be at loggerheads it can only be because theology is trying to shore up pre-scientific ways of doing theology by utilizing uncritical methods of reading the Bible. Criticism is the fine-tuning of knowledge, the winnowing of the chaff from the wheat, and the putting into perspective of what can be known. Why should theology have any difficulties with such processes? If half the energy which some theologians devote to reconciling (integrating?) modern science with religion were put into integrating biblical criticism and theology, intelligent critical theology might be in better shape today.

The problematics outlined in this book might remain at some level, but they might also contribute to a seriously dialectical account of how theology and Bible could be worked together. Both would have to make serious concessions to each other, and the developing consensus – if such were possible – would probably look nothing like earlier and more traditional forms of theology. Problems would always remain because the two are not the same, and there are powerful tensions which are never going to be resolved.

The level of generality in this book should not conceal from the reader that there are many individual examples of intelligent theology being done in the world today – theology which has taken the measure of the critical reading of the Bible and integrated it into theology as much as it will integrate. If I do not mention any specific names, it is because I do not wish to enforce any pack-drill formations. At some level, I suspect, theology and Bible will always operate on opposite sides of a divide which cannot be overcome permanently. The diversity of scripture will generate competing theological interpretations, and theology will never be able to develop all these different viewpoints into one grand theory. Nor should it need to do so. The multitudinous number of churches and religious communities in the world today which use the Bible at various levels is ample evidence of the diversity of scripture. Some communities have little use for the Bible, others have less use for theology. Pluralistic practices and interpretations are guaranteed for ever!

My final observation is this. With so many different competing views of the Bible in the world, and such variety of opinion about whether the Bible is important or not, or in what sense it is important or otherwise, the individual reader may find it easier to treat the Bible *as a book* – ideally as a collection of books – and to read it as such. Assuming a high degree of literacy and a sophisticated eye/ear for the subtlety of nuance in the book, the reader will enter a strange world unlike anything in the West today. How the reader's adventures in that weird world will affect their lives or minds cannot be predicted. It is unpredictable because when the imagination is let loose on the imaginative productions of human culture, anything can happen. If the reader happens to be religious, then perhaps a warning should be given. Whatever you may imagine the gods are like, what you will encounter in the Bible will be different. Wind and fire, whirlwinds and volcanoes, silences and quiet voices will depict aspects of the divine which will be well beyond your control. Encounters with and accounts of the transcendental will beggar your vocabulary. Metaphors will spin out of control and images will haunt the mind for weeks. Irony will keep you sane, but human stupidity as depicted in its pages will hold a mirror up to you. Its critique of power relations and its accounts of the oppressed will make you mistrust any organized religion to which you may belong. If you read the book in the company of a good exegete/reader you will gain much but be warned again that even such may have feet of clay. Reflecting on what you read may not be as conducive to systematic thought as you might have wished. The book is too untidy, too sprawling and far too boisterous to be tamed by neat systems of thought. If you want neatness, close the book and turn to theology. But if you can tolerate contradiction and contrariety and can handle hyperbolic drive and chaotic manipulation of metaphor, then the Bible will burn your mind. We humans have produced few things like it. Oh, and a final word of warning: 'The things that you're liable to read in the Bible . . . ain't necessarily so!'

Bibliographical Notes

These Notes are intended to supply the reader with information on the sources of the epigraphs used throughout the book, to indicate the location of any quotations in the text, and to supply background information relevant to the arguments of each chapter.

General epigraphs: S. Kierkegaard, *Concluding Unscientific Postscript* (Princeton, NJ, Princeton University Press, 1968), p. 260; F. Nietzsche, *The Will to Power* (Vintage Books 1968), §241, p. 139; W. Benjamin, 'Theses on the Philosophy of History', English version in H. Arendt ed., *Illuminations* (Collins 1973), p. 258; W. Stevens, 'An Ordinary Evening in New Haven: XIX', *Collected Poems* (Faber 1984), p. 479; N. Frye, *The Great Code: The Bible and literature* (Routledge & Kegan Paul 1982), p. xviii.

INTRODUCTION

W. Stevens, 'Conversation with Three Women of New England', *Opus Posthumous* (Vintage Books 1989), p. 134; J. Derrida, *Of Grammatology* (Baltimore, MD, Johns Hopkins University Press, 1976), p. 102.

CHAPTER ONE   THE BOOK OF BOOKS

Epigraph: E. Pound, *The Cantos of Ezra Pound* (Faber 1975), Canto LXXIV, p. 430. An invaluable aid to understanding the complexities of translation is G. Steiner, *After Babel: Aspects of language and translation* (Oxford University Press 1975); for Auerbach see E. Auerbach, *Mimesis: The representation of reality in Western literature* (Princeton University Press 1953), chs. 1 and 2. On the opacity of language in the Bible see S. Prickett, *Words and The Word: Language, poetics and biblical interpretation* (Cambridge University Press 1986); on 'Judaisms' see the multitudinous writings of Jacob Neusner. As an introduction to *Rezeptionsgeschichte* of the Bible see the three-volume *Cambridge History of the Bible* (Cambridge University Press 1970); a briefer and more elementary approach may be found in R. J. Coggins & J. L. Houlden, eds, *A Dictionary of Biblical Interpretation* (SCM 1990). A most useful introduction to the rise of the critical method is K. Scholder, *The Birth of Modern Critical Theology: Origins and problems of biblical criticism in the seventeenth century* (SCM 1990); on the impact of the critical approach to the study of Jesus see J. Bowden, *Jesus: The unanswered questions* (SCM 1988). The emic/etic distinction is discussed at length in K. Pike, *Language in Relation to a Unified Theory* (Mouton & Co. 1967²), pp. 37–72.

CHAPTER TWO   GOD THE HIDDEN PROBLEMATIC

Epigraphs: B. Pascal, *Pensées* (Penguin Classics 1966), no. 242, p. 103; cf. *Pascal: Oeuvres complètes* (Paris, Éditions du Séuil, 1963), p. 531; K. Barth, *Church Dogmatics* II/1 (Edinburgh, T. & T. Clark, 1957), p. 183. For the

BIBLIOGRAPHICAL NOTES

Christendom background see J. Herrin, *The Formation of Christendom* (Blackwell 1987); on Pascal's thought see L. Goldmann, *The Hidden God* (Routledge & Kegan Paul 1964) and S. E. Melzer, *Discourses of the Fall: A study of Pascal's Pensées* (Berkeley, CA, University of California Press, 1986). On Yahweh as a character in a story see B. Wicker, *The Story-Shaped World. Fiction and Metaphysics: Some variations on a theme* (The Athlone Press 1975), pp. 71–106; on the origins of Satan see N. Forsyth, *The Old Enemy: Satan and the combat myth* (Princeton, NJ, Princeton University Press, 1987) – Forsyth's allusion to J. Edgar Hoover appears on p. 115. For the technical details of the biblical metaphor see S. E. Balentine, *The Hidden God: The hiding of the face of God in the Old Testament* (Oxford University Press 1983); for theological possibilities in the theme see S. Terrien, *The Elusive Presence: Toward a new biblical theology* (New York, Harper & Row, 1978); a useful treatment of the motif in relation to Christian theology is D. Cupitt, *Christ and the Hiddenness of God* (Lutterworth Press 1971). On Spinoza's contribution see B. Spinoza, *Tractatus Theologico-Politicus* (1670); there are numerous English translations available of this work.

CHAPTER THREE   THE CHIMERA OF BIBLICAL CHRISTIANITY

Epigraphs: M. Twain, *Europe and Elsewhere* (Harper & Brothers 1923), p. 387; M. Arnold, 'Letter to his Mother: 25 June 1870' in G.W.E. Russell ed., *Letters of Matthew Arnold 1848–1888* (Macmillan 1895), vol. ii, p. 36; V. van Gogh, letter cited in T. Kodera, *Vincent van Gogh: Christianity versus nature* (Philadelphia, John Benjamins, 1990), p. 49. M. Twain's short chapter 'Bible Teaching and Religious Practice' (*Europe and Elsewhere*, pp. 387–393) contains an excellent statement of the principle, 'The text remains, the practice changes.' On some fundamentalist uses of the Bible see K.C. Boone, *The Bible Tells Them So: The discourse of Protestant fundamentalism* (SCM 1990); any competent anthology of the writings of J.L. Borges should contain his 'The Don Quixote of Pierre Menard'. For the influence of K. Marx on this chapter see his famous pamphlet 'The Eighteenth Brumaire of Louis Bonaparte', available in most reliable anthologies of Marx's writings (e.g. D. McLellen ed., *Karl Marx: Selected writings* (Oxford University Press 1977), pp. 300–325); on early Christian views of sex see P. Brown, *The Body and Society: Men, women and sexual renunciation in early Christianity* (Faber 1989); on attitudes to homosexuality see J. Boswell, *Christianity, Social Tolerance, and Homosexuality: Gay people in western Europe from the beginning of the Christian era to the fourteenth century* (University of Chicago Press 1980); on sex in the New Testament see L.W. Countryman, *Dirt, Greed and Sex: Sexual ethics in the New Testament and their implications for today* (SCM 1989); on more general issues see J.T. Sanders, *Ethics in the New Testament: Change and development* (SCM 1986). See also H. Räisänen, *Beyond New Testament Theology: A story and a programme* (SCM 1990). On Newman's book see J.H. Newman, *An Essay on the Development of Christian Doctrine*, ed. J.M. Cameron (Penguin 1974). C. Evans's important essay 'Is "Holy Scripture" Christian?' appears in his collection *Is 'Holy Scripture' Christian? and other questions* (SCM 1971), pp. 21–36; his essay 'Is the New Testament Church a Model?' in the same collection (pp. 78–90) also bears on this chapter's concerns. On the Scottish Free Church experience of biblical criticism see R.A. Riesen, *Criticism and Faith in Late Victorian Scotland: A.B. Davidson, William Robertson Smith and George Adam Smith* (Lanham, MD, University Press of America, 1985).

CHAPTER FOUR   THE PEOPLE OF THE JEWS

Epigraphs: H. Melville, 'January 1857' in *Journals* (Evanston, IL, Northwestern University Press, 1989), p. 91; E. Jabès, *The Book of Questions: Yaël, Elya, Aely* (Middletown, CT, Wesleyan University Press, 1983), p. 143; W.B. Yeats, 'Two Songs from a Play', *Collected Poems* (Macmillan 1965), p. 240. As background to this chapter see J.G. Gager, *The Origins of Anti-Semitism: Attitudes toward Judaism in pagan and Christian antiquity* (Oxford University Press 1983). Details of the Shoah are adequately documented by R. Hilberg, *The Destruction of the European Jews*, 3 vols. (New York, Holmes & Meier, 1985); see also R.L. Rubenstein and J.K. Roth, *Approaches to Auschwitz: The legacy of the Holocaust* (SCM 1987). A most important essay on the subject is I. Greenberg's 'Cloud of Smoke, Pillar of Fire: Judaism, Christianity, and Modernity after the Holocaust' in E. Fleischner ed., *Auschwitz: Beginning of a New Era? Reflections on the Holocaust* (Hoboken, NJ, KTAV, 1977), pp. 7–55. On the New Testament handling of Jewish scripture see B. Lindars, *New Testament Apologetic: The doctrinal significance of the Old Testament quotations* (SCM 1961); for the later Jewish polemic see O.S. Rankin, *Jewish Religious Polemic of Early and Later Centuries: A study of documents here rendered in English* (Edinburgh University Press 1956), the Ramban quotation is from p. 208. On secrecy in the Gospels see F. Kermode, *The Genesis of Secrecy: On the interpretation of narrative* (Cambridge, MA, Harvard University Press, 1979).

CHAPTER FIVE   WOLF IN SHEEP'S CLOTHING

Epigraphs: F. Kafka, 'Letter to Oskar Pollak: 27 January 1904' (see *Briefe 1902-1924* [S. Fischer Verlag 1958] pp. 27f.) cf. F. Kafka, *Letters to Friends, Family, & Editors* trs. R. & C. Winston (Schocken Books 1977), pp. 15f.; R.M. Rilke, 'Archaic Torso of Apollo' in *Selected Works*: vol.2 *Poetry* (The Hogarth Press 1960), p. 143. I have used the Penguin Classics translation (by R.S. Pine-Coffin) of Augustine's *Confessions* (1961) and the Loeb Classical Library Latin edition (translation by W. Watts, 1912); a good guide to Augustine is P. Brown, *Augustine of Hippo: A biography* (Faber 1967). For Bunyan see the Penguin English Library edition of *The Pilgrim's Progress*, ed. R. Sharrock (1965); an excellent treatment of Bunyan is C. Hill, *A Turbulent, Seditious, and Factious People: John Bunyan and his Church 1628-1688* (Oxford University Press 1988). The inscribed Bible found at Majdanek (a similar one had been found in Aix-en-Provence six hundred years before) is referred to in D.G. Roskies, *Against the Apocalypse: Responses to catastrophe in modern Jewish culture* (Cambridge, MA, Harvard University Press, 1984), p. 249. For general matters see E.P. Sanders, *Jesus and Judaism* (SCM 1985). On the poverty of Jesus see U. Eco, *The Name of the Rose* (Picador 1984), pp. 335–348. On the immediacy of literature see G. Steiner, *Real Presences: Is there anything in what we say?* (Faber 1989). On

BIBLIOGRAPHICAL NOTES

Moody and Sankey see D.M. Robertson, *The Chicago Revival, 1876: Society and revivalism in a nineteenth-century city* (Metuchen, NJ, The Scarecrow Press, 1989); quotation from pp. 158f. The Auden quote is from his poem 'Under Which Lyre' in W.H. Auden, *Collected Shorter Poems 1927–1957* (Faber 1966), p. 226.

CONCLUSION

R. Browning, 'Bishop Bloughram's Apology' lines 581–584 in R. Browning, *The Poems, Volume I*, ed. J. Pettigrew (Penguin 1981), p. 632. The Blake poem quoted from is 'The Everlasting Gospel' lines 13–14 in *Blake: Complete Writings*, ed. G. Keynes (Oxford University Press 1969), p. 748. My closing lines are from Gershwin's *Porgy and Bess*.

Select Bibliography

R. Alter and F. Kermode, eds, *The Literary Guide to the Bible* (Collins 1987)

J. Barr, *The Bible in the Modern World* (SCM 1973)

J. Barton, *People of the Book? The authority of the Bible in Christianity* (SPCK 1988)

R.B. Coote and M.P. Coote, *Power, Politics, and the Making of the Bible: An introduction* (Philadelphia, Fortress, 1990)

J. Drury, ed., *Critics of the Bible 1724–1873* (Cambridge University Press 1989)

H. Fisch, *Poetry With a Purpose: Biblical poetics and interpretation* (Bloomington, IN, Indiana University Press, 1988)

H.W. Frei, *The Eclipse of Biblical Narrative: A study of eighteenth and nineteenth-century hermeneutics* (New Haven, CT, Yale University Press, 1974)

R.P.C. Hanson and A.T. Hanson, *The Bible without Illusions* (SCM 1989)

D.H. Kelsey, *The Uses of Scripture in Recent Theology* (SCM 1975)

R. Morgan with J. Barton, *Biblical Interpretation* (Oxford University Press 1988)

D. Nineham, *The Use and Abuse of the Bible: A study of the Bible in an age of rapid cultural change* (SPCK 1978)

R.A. Oden, *The Bible Without Theology: The theological tradition and alternatives to it* (New York, Harper & Row, 1987)

J.K.S. Reid, *The Authority of Scripture: A study of the Reformation and Post-Reformation understanding of the Bible* (Methuen 1957)

P. Ricoeur, *Essays on Biblical Interpretation* (SPCK 1981)

R.M. Schwartz, ed., *The Book and the Text: The Bible and literary theory* (Blackwell 1990)

S. Smalley, *The Study of the Bible in the Middle Ages* (Blackwell 1984³)

M. Sternberg, *The Poetics of Biblical Narrative: Ideological literature and the drama of reading* (Bloomington, IN, Indiana University Press, 1985)

Index of Biblical References

INDEX OF BIBLICAL REFERENCES

Index of Names

INDEX OF NAMES

Index of Subjects

INDEX OF SUBJECTS